Penguin Monarchs

* Now in paperback

ROSEMARY HORROX

Richard III

A Failed King?

ALLEN LANE
an imprint of
PENGUIN BOOKS

ALLEN LANE

UK | USA | Canada | Ireland | Australia
India | New Zealand | South Africa

Penguin Books is part of the Penguin Random House group of companies
whose addresses can be found at global.penguinrandomhouse.com

First published 2020
001

Copyright © Rosemary Horrox, 2020

The moral right of the author has been asserted

Set in 9.5/13.5 pt Sabon LT Std
Typeset by Jouve (UK), Milton Keynes
Printed and bound in Great Britain by Clays Ltd, Elcograf S.p.A.

ISBN: 978-0-141-97893-2

www.greenpenguin.co.uk

Contents

To Tybert the Cat
and his predecessors,
who may look at a king

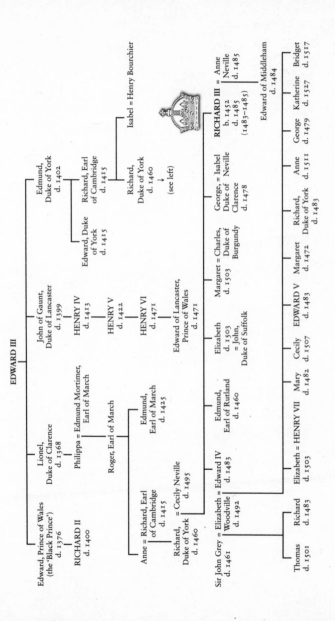

EDWARD III

Edward, Prince of Wales (the 'Black Prince') d. 1376

RICHARD II d. 1400

Lionel, Duke of Clarence d. 1368

Philippa = Edmund Mortimer, Earl of March

Roger, Earl of March

Edmund, Earl of March d. 1425

Anne = Richard, Earl of Cambridge d. 1415

Richard, Duke of York d. 1460 = Cecily Neville d. 1495

John of Gaunt, Duke of Lancaster d. 1399

HENRY IV d. 1413

HENRY V d. 1422

HENRY VI d. 1471

Edward of Lancaster, Prince of Wales d. 1471

Edmund, Duke of York d. 1402

Richard, Earl of Cambridge d. 1415

Edward, Duke of York d. 1415

Richard, Duke of York d. 1460 → (see left)

Isabel = Henry Bourchier

Edmund, Earl of Rutland d. 1460

Sir John Grey = Elizabeth Woodville d. 1492
d. 1461

Thomas d. 1501

Richard d. 1483

Elizabeth = HENRY VII d. 1503
d. 1503

Mary d. 1482

Cecily d. 1507

EDWARD V d. 1483

Elizabeth d. 1503 = John, Duke of Suffolk

Margaret = Charles, Duke of Burgundy d. 1503

Margaret d. 1472

Richard, Duke of York d. 1483

George, = Isabel Neville Duke of Clarence d. 1478

RICHARD III = Anne Neville b. 1452 d. 1485
d. 1485 (1483–1485)

Edward of Middleham d. 1484

George d. 1479

Katherine d. 1527

Bridget d. 1517

Anne d. 1511

Elizabeth = Edward IV d. 1483

Richard III

Prologue

On 22 August 1485, Richard III died at Bosworth. Crowned at Westminster on 6 July 1483, he had been King of England for just two years and forty-seven days: still the shortest reign of any crowned post-Conquest ruler of England. He was the first, and was to be the last, King of England to die in battle since Harold; but, unlike Harold, he died fighting his own subjects. His death also put an end to the Yorkist dynasty established by his brother Edward in 1461. By any utilitarian measure this has to be regarded as a failure: monarchs were, and indeed still are, expected to hang on to their throne and hand it on safely to the next heir. Richard's death in battle denied him even the shadowy post-mortem existence of the murdered Edward II and Richard II. Ricardian loyalists, though, continued to cause trouble for the Tudors. Writing in the early seventeenth century about the reign of Henry VII, Francis Bacon thought that the memory of Richard was 'so strong that it lay like lees in the bottom of men's hearts, and if the vessel were but stirred it would come up'.[1] But the dead king's surrogates, his nephews the Earls of Warwick and Lincoln, were in truth unpersuasive.

The question mark in this book's subtitle is not, however, entirely redundant. Richard III is unique among English medieval kings in the passion he arouses among his defenders. Much of that passion has been directed against the image of the king elaborated in Tudor polemic and embodied in Shakespeare's first tetralogy, the three *Henry VI* plays and *Richard III* : the smiling, amoral, hunchbacked villain who hacked his way to the throne. No historian now takes that model seriously. One question that still hangs over the reign might, however, be seen as a faint reflection of that earlier quarrel. To what extent were the events that followed the death of Edward IV and culminated in Richard's accession driven by the latter's own desires, or were they the ineluctable consequence of a profoundly dysfunctional Yorkist regime, of which Richard was more victim than villain?

Once Richard had been crowned he was the Lord's anointed, to whom earthly obedience was due. There was no period of the Middle Ages when kings were exempt from criticism, but armed opposition, of the sort that faced Richard III, raised different and more difficult issues. Why were hitherto loyal Yorkists prepared to turn so decisively against him, and thereby ultimately against the dynasty itself? Neither of the questions posed here has an uncontested answer.

I
The Youngest Brother

The future Richard III was born at Fotheringhay (North-amptonshire) on 2 October 1452, the fourth son, and last surviving child, of Richard, Duke of York, and Cecily Neville. He was born into a country confronting the certainty of final defeat in its hundred years of war with France, and about to collapse into a civil war at home. Political tensions within the English ruling elite were rapidly becoming unsustainable. The inadequacies of Henry VI had long been obvious; now, rifts within the circle around the king were widening dangerously, setting Richard's father in opposition to the Beauforts, the king's family of the half-blood, and, increasingly, to Henry's queen, Margaret of Anjou. The king's complete mental collapse in the summer of 1453 brought the problems out into the open, and his apparent recovery at the very end of the following year did nothing to resolve them. On 22 May 1455, at St Albans, the Duke of York and his supporters launched an attack on the royal party after negotiations between them had broken down. With hindsight this episode, in which several of Henry's closest allies were killed, can be seen as the first move in the Wars of the Roses, although York was still protesting his loyalty to the crown and casting himself only as the opponent of the 'evil counsellors' around the king. After this the genie could not be put back into the bottle and, in spite of intermittent and ineffectual peace-making efforts, both sides prepared for war. In October 1459, York confronted the royal army outside Ludlow, where his forces, faced by the presence of the king in person, refused to fight. The duke, his two eldest sons and their ally the Earl of Warwick fled into exile. In their absence they and their leading supporters were condemned as trai-tors in the so-called 'parliament of devils', and their land seized. The only way out of the impasse left for York was to claim the throne, and in autumn 1460 he returned to do just that.

York's insistence before parliament that his claim out-ranked that of the house of Lancaster because it derived from his descent from Edward III's second son Lionel, Duke of Clarence, albeit in the female line, evidently caused the Lords acute embarrassment. After much attempted buck-passing, an agreement was brokered that Henry should remain king for his lifetime, with York and his heirs then succeeding. The disinheriting of her son Edward, the Prince of Wales, was never going to be acceptable to Queen Margaret, and both sides began to raise troops. At the end of the year her army defeated York's forces at Wakefield, where both the duke and his second son, Edmund, were killed. The Lancastrian army then headed south for Lon-don. When news of their father's defeat reached the city, the eight-year-old Richard and his two elder siblings, George and Margaret, were hastily packed off across the Channel to the safekeeping of the Duke of Burgundy.

By the time they returned to England in June 1461, the situation had been transformed. At the beginning of February, York's heir Edward, then aged eighteen, had defeated a Lancastrian army at Mortimer's Cross in Shropshire. He followed up his victory by marching on London, where he was proclaimed king on 4 March. On 29 March, Edward IV's assumption of the throne was confirmed by his decisive victory at Towton (North Yorkshire). This changed his young brothers' status dramatically – underlined by their move into the ducal palace at Bruges for the remainder of their stay in Burgundian territory. George was now his brother's heir, Richard 'the spare'. Both were made dukes: George 'of Clarence' on the day of Edward's coronation; Richard 'of Gloucester' five months later. But for the next seven years or so Richard is largely invisible, except as the recipient of royal grants of land and office – both on a significantly smaller scale than those amassed by his elder brother George or, indeed, by a number of Edward's other allies. He is not much on historians' radar screens in these years, and nor – still overshadowed by his brother George, the heir – does he seem to have been fully on the king's.

Towards the end of 1465, when he had turned thirteen, Richard entered the household of his cousin Richard Neville, Earl of Warwick – a leading ally of the house of York since the mid 1450s. Neville's own territorial interests lay predominantly in the north-east, but thanks to the addition of his wife's combined Despenser and Beauchamp inheritance (and the winnowing of the Lancastrian aristocracy) he was now territorially the most powerful English magnate of his day. Once in the earl's keeping, Richard

7

largely drops from sight again, apparently tucked away in
the north while Edward's regime slipped towards crisis.

Edward's first parliament in November 1461 had begun
with two major items of business. The second was confirmation of the house of York's title to the throne.
Precedence on the parliament roll, however, was given to
the Commons' fulsome commendation of Edward's action
in rescuing the realm from the 'extortion, murder, rape,
the shedding of innocent blood, riot and unrighteousness'
of the previous regime.[1] The reign of Henry VI had been a
disaster and his replacement by a young, personable king
seemed in the euphoria of the moment to promise a new
beginning. This inevitably proved over-optimistic. The
cause of Lancaster was very far from lost, and several of its
leaders who had initially made their peace with the new
regime and been pardoned subsequently reneged. The
problem was at first compounded by the deposed king's
survival at large. He was finally captured and imprisoned
in July 1465; kept alive to prevent the title to the throne
passing to his son – safely out of Edward's reach in exile
with his mother, Queen Margaret of Anjou, in France. In
the event, however, it was to be division within the Yorkist
establishment that offered renewal of the dwindling Lancastrian interest.

On 1 May 1464, Edward had married, in secret, Elizabeth Woodville, widow of the Lancastrian John Grey,
Lord Ferrers. Virtually every commentator, then and now,
has regarded the Woodville marriage as toxic. It threw away
the diplomatic opportunities represented by a bachelor king

at a time when the new dynasty was seeking European allies. The marriage was taken as a personal insult by Warwick, who was negotiating for a French marriage at the time and, like the rest of the political community, was only told about the wedding the following autumn. It also injected a new element into English domestic politics. Elizabeth had two sons by her first marriage, and five brothers and seven sisters, only one of whom – her eldest brother, Anthony – was already married. This immediately placed a potential burden on royal patronage that a foreign marriage would not. Edward engineered aristocratic marriages for the sisters, which cost him relatively little and might also have served to bind their husbands securely to the royal interest, but making provision for the queen's male kin would potentially require more outlay. Cost apart, the extension of the royal family also brought a significant shift in the balance of the circle around the king – those who had the king's ear.

The mopping up of available aristocratic husbands had practical consequences for Warwick, whose heirs were his two daughters. His proposed solution – that the Duke of Clarence should marry the eldest daughter, Isabel – was promptly vetoed by the king. It made sense for Edward to keep his brothers' marriages as diplomatic bargaining chips, but the rebuff was taken by Warwick, no doubt correctly, as a demonstration that he could no longer presume on his former influence over the king. Clarence, whose status as his brother's heir was now looking distinctly short-term, drew the same conclusion. In 1469 duke and earl moved into overt opposition to the crown. At the beginning of

July, against a background of local unrest in the north-east (in which Warwick certainly had a hand), the duke was married to Isabel in Calais. From there, the two lords issued a manifesto explicitly likening the failings of Edward's regime to those of the three previously deposed English monarchs and calling upon their supporters to join them in arms.[2] Royal and rebel forces fought at Edgecote (Buckinghamshire) on 25 July, and the latter were victorious. In the battle's aftermath, the queen's father Earl Rivers and her youngest brother John were among those executed, without legal process. Edward, not present at the battle itself, was subsequently captured and imprisoned at Warwick's North Yorkshire base of Middleham. In London, Clarence, along with Warwick's brother George, the Archbishop of York, tried to keep the show on the road in the face of a significant breakdown in public order. The task proved impossible, and in October the king returned, unchallenged, to London.

It is across this period that Richard begins to come more clearly into view. He had apparently left the Earl of Warwick's household towards the end of 1468, when he turned sixteen. Early in 1469 he was in Edward's company as the royal court moved round the country, and although he is still largely invisible in contemporary chronicles, those in the know already recognized him as someone well placed to exercise 'good lordship' and advance their interests.[3] The king also seems to have awoken to the need to find his youngest brother a proper landed endowment. Richard's existing ducal holdings were a ragbag collection which provided no coherent regional power base. Little was now left of the windfall Lancastrian forfeitures from the early years of the reign, and it is indicative of the importance which Edward now attached to the issue that he resorted to dismembering the duchy of Lancaster – the massive collection of land brought into the crown by Henry IV – on his brother's behalf. In May 1469, Richard was given, during the king's pleasure, a major grant of duchy land in Lancashire and Cheshire, together with all rights and offices in the land concerned. This grant, which cut sharply across the regional authority of the powerful Thomas, Lord Stanley, generated the first manifestation of what was to be an enduring conflict of interest when Richard promptly aligned himself with the Harrington family in their local dispute with the Stanleys.[4]

The execution of leading royal allies in the aftermath of Edgecote replenished the store of available patronage, their titles and lands reverting to the crown. So, to an even greater extent, did the subsequent defection of Clarence and Warwick in spring 1470. Richard was among the beneficiaries in both cases, and although the initial hasty redistribution of the spoils looks like an emergency quick fix, his gains show that he was now to be trusted with significant authority. He was made constable of England in place of the executed Earl Rivers, and was lined up as the replacement for William Herbert, Earl of Pembroke, another Edwardian loyalist and victim of Edgecote, in Wales and the Marches. In August 1470, Richard replaced Warwick as warden of the West March towards Scotland, thereby acquiring quasi-royal authority in England's north-western borderlands, although the earl's other key offices went elsewhere.

By the time of that August grant to Richard, his brother Clarence together with Warwick had thrown in their lot with the house of Lancaster. In February 1470 a local rising had flared up in Lincolnshire, which, according to the official account of events, was utilized by Clarence to stage an explicit bid for the throne.[5] Whatever the truth of this, and the account as it stands begs some questions, the nerve of Clarence and Warwick clearly broke as the king raised troops to quell the rising. The Lincolnshire rebels were defeated and the two lords, without themselves engaging the royal army, fled to France. Here Warwick embraced the cause of Henry VI's restoration. His second daughter, Anne, was betrothed to Prince Edward of Lancaster in the cathedral at Angers on 25 July. In September their forces invaded England, and Edward, with his leading allies, including Richard, was driven into exile in the Low Countries.

The re-accession of Henry VI proved unpersuasive. The Lancastrian king was in a poor mental and physical state, and Queen Margaret and her son refused to cross to England until his restoration seemed assured. By the time they did arrive, Edward IV had invaded with Burgundian backing; Clarence had, predictably perhaps, jumped ship, returning to his brothers' side; and Warwick and his forces had been defeated at Barnet, north of London, where the earl was among the dead. The massacre of Margaret's army at Tewkesbury, with the killing there of Edward of Lancaster, and the subsequent death of Henry VI in the Tower (implausibly ascribed by a Yorkist source to 'pure displeasure and melancholy')[6] following hard upon the Yorkists' return to London, clinched the destruction of the house of Lancaster and put Edward on the throne for a second time.

The past decade had seen kingship treated as negotiable. Individuals might still display deep commitment to one side or the other, but who was sitting on the throne had become in practice contingent on aristocratic power struggles (plus, latterly, foreign backing). Deposition had become an easier option (and, strikingly, no longer had to be camouflaged as a voluntary abdication, as had been the case with Edward II and Richard II). This can largely be explained by the concurrent existence until May 1471 of two anointed kings. The crown was not literally up for grabs – and if in 1470 Clarence had indeed thought that it was, he had been proved wrong. Yet the period had brought unsettling evidence of a new precariousness in a king's right to power. A role that should have been unassailable had acquired a dangerous air of provisionality.

Edward's resumption of the throne in 1471 was regarded by contemporaries as drawing a line under the upheavals of the previous decade. The Lancastrian claim to the throne had been decisively extinguished, and Edward now had the luxury of rethinking the rather ad hoc distribution of regional authority in the last couple of years. The suggestion in 1469 that Richard might take up William Herbert's role as the king's 'master-lock' in Wales was now shelved. Instead, he stepped swiftly into the dead Warwick's northern hegemony – a policy which, given the rapidity with which the first grants followed Edward's return, had probably been decided in principle before he regained the throne. The duke received the earl's northern castles of Middleham, Sheriff Hutton and Penrith in late June 1471, superseded a fortnight later by a more comprehensively worded grant of all the Neville lands in Yorkshire and Cumberland. To his existing wardenship of the West March Richard now added the crucial role of chief steward of the duchy of Lancaster in the north, which extended his reach well beyond his own landed base west into Lancashire and south into the Midlands.

Richard's assumption of Warwick's power has an air of inevitability, as does his intention to marry the earl's younger daughter and co-heiress, Anne, now a fifteen-year-old widow following the death of her husband, Prince Edward of Lancaster. Clarence objected fiercely to the marriage, reputedly to the extent of hiding Anne by disguising her as a kitchen-maid, but was finally persuaded by the king to agree and the requisite papal indulgence was granted on 22 April 1472.[7] Clarence still sulkily resisted plans to allow Anne any share of her father's land and the division of Warwick's inheritance between the two brothers was only finally agreed after considerable pressure had been brought to bear on him. Broadly speaking, Clarence secured the southern lands, including those of the former Beauchamp earls of Warwick, and Richard the northern. Both brothers were united, though, on one thing: that they should hold the land by right of marriage and not through royal grant, which would be inherently more vulnerable. This meant that Warwick (along with his followers) escaped parliamentary attainder, with its concomitant forfeiture. The settlement as concluded also stripped his widow of her existing rights in the land she had brought to the marriage, in spite of her pleas for justice.[8]

The three northern Neville lordships, plus the Beauchamp lordship of Barnard Castle in County Durham, were to constitute the heart of Richard's northern power base. In all four he was able to step into the leadership of an existing following; a relationship smoothed, perhaps, by his marriage to Warwick's daughter. In the course of the 1470s he worked outwards from that base to widen his connection beyond that of the earl by brokering deals that traded estates marginal to his northern interests for more strategically valuable ones. Scarborough (a royal castle and manor) was acquired in this way, as was the Clifford barony in the West Riding centred on Skipton and Craven. After the conviction for treason and execution of Clarence in 1478, Richard surrendered earlier royal grants in the West Country in exchange for his dead brother's lands in Yorkshire, including the long-coveted castle of Richmond. This had initially been granted to Richard in 1462, but at that stage quickly taken back and conferred on Clarence when he staked a claim to it.

By the mid 1470s, Richard was by far the dominant figure in northern England, pulling lesser lords into his orbit, among them the Scropes of Masham and the FitzHughs of Ravensworth. This was at the expense of the Percy earls of Northumberland, the leading regional family in the first half of the century. They had been eclipsed during most of Edward IV's first reign, but restored to the earldom by him in 1470, probably as a counterbalance to Warwick as he moved into opposition. Now their marginalization was marked enough to come to the notice of the royal council in 1473. Richard was made to promise that he would be the Earl of Northumberland's good and faithful lord, and would not claim any office or fee granted to the earl, or take any of the earl's retainers into his service: an agreement embodied the following year in an indenture between the two men.[9] This recognized the Duke of Gloucester's primacy, while limiting his encroachment on Percy interests. Richard seems to have kept the letter of his promise, although sons and brothers of Percy retainers did continue to enter his service. If the implication of the agreement is that Richard had previously been engaging in some aggressive empire-building, it also suggests that the earl's retainers may have recognized the superior value of ducal lordship.

That lordship was valued by the king as well. An expanded ducal connection in the north, with Richard effectively acting as the king's proxy, had the potential to harmonize a formerly divided and fractious region: to make it 'sit still and be quiet'.[10] This was Edward's aim, and he was correspondingly willing to facilitate the consolidation of his brother's power. The exchanges of land could not have been made without his agreement and it is unlikely that they demonstrate only a lazy indulgence of his brother's demands. Edward was not altogether prepared to give Richard his head, and the influence of Thomas, Lord Stanley, in the duchy lands in Lancashire continued to be protected in the 1470s, in spite of Richard's chief stewardship. But the duke should not be seen simply as an embodiment of royal authority. The power he was amassing was his to use; the men who looked to him for lordship were *his* men – even, as would become apparent, the members of the royal household within his circle. While Edward IV lived there was no conflict of interest. What was good for one brother was good for the other; although the council of the duchy of Lancaster might grumble at times about the administrative negligence of some of the duke's associates.[11]

The north was the crucial element in Richard's power, and the one to which he was most attentive, but it did not mark the geographical limits of his authority. Simultaneously constable and admiral of England, his writ ran throughout the country. Neither office was a sinecure, although they could be delegated. The military and chivalric jurisdiction of the former might also entail investigating accusations of treason in peacetime. The latter role brought influence in ports throughout the realm. Richard also held land outside the north; albeit a shifting collection that was on the whole too scattered to allow the development of an extended retinue, although it might have brought useful local contacts. The exception to this pattern was East Anglia, where Richard did for a time aim at more of a presence through his acquisition of the de Vere lands there. He had held them nominally and very briefly after the execution of John de Vere, 12th Earl of Oxford, in 1462 and regained them after their forfeiture by John, the 13th Earl, in 1471. He followed this up by successfully pressuring the widow of the 12th Earl to make over her dower lands to him; but in 1475, in a territorial reshuffling probably brokered by the king, Richard surrendered the de Veres'

Suffolk estates and their most important Essex properties to Edward's queen, Elizabeth Woodville, and her feoffees (trustees) as a pendant to her existing interest in the duchy of Lancaster lands in the region.[12]

As the Duke of Gloucester waxed, his elder brother and rival waned. Although Clarence had rejoined his brothers on their return to England in March 1471 and had fought beside them at Barnet and Tewkesbury, he seems never quite to have shaken off the stigma of disloyalty. The cause of Lancaster – or at least of opposition to York – still had a few flickers of life in the 1470s and it may well be that Clarence was still dabbling in treason; although his fierce opposition to the dismemberment of the Warwick inheritance would have probably been enough by itself to sink him in Edward's estimation. Either way, it was not very long after Edward's restoration that Clarence's power began to be eroded. The most visible evidence of this came when he was denied exemption from a parliamentary Act of Resumption in October 1473 and was thereby stripped at a stroke of all his royal grants. This was designed to be the final turn of the screw to force him to agreement with Richard over the Warwick inheritance, but settlement of the dispute brought only a partial restoration of Clarence's former grants and the nibbling away at his power continued.

Clarence's final downfall played out across 1477, culminating in Edward's decision to put him on trial for treason. Because the duke had the right to be tried by his peers, parliament was summoned to meet on 16 January 1478. Nothing about the trial appears on the parliament roll itself, although a list of the accusations survives, as does the appointment of the Duke of Buckingham as High Steward to pronounce sentence on 7 February. Contemporary observers were deeply shocked by the trial. Only the king spoke against his brother, only Clarence answered; the witnesses, it was reported, behaved more like accusers.[13] At the end, Clarence offered to prove his innocence by personal combat, which was refused. Unsurprisingly he was found guilty, although the king then hesitated over signing the order for his execution and needed to be told by the Speaker of the Commons to get on with it. He was put to death, privately, in the Tower of London on 20 February.

Clarence's fall was later to be seized upon by Shakespeare and others as an early example of Richard's evil machinations. Some writers at the time, and most of the recent commentators on the episode, have been more inclined to take it as *prima facie* evidence of a dangerously dysfunctional and factionalized power structure within the Yorkist court, with the Woodvilles now more likely to be seen as the villains of the piece. Certainly the Woodvilles and their allies had been the primary target for Clarence and Warwick's disaffection in 1469, and their manifesto had had very rude things to say about the 'disceyvabille covetous rule and gydynge of certeyne ceducious persons . . . only entendyng to thaire owen promocion and enrichyng'.[14] The battle-lines between 'ins' and 'outs' were to be less explicitly articulated in Edward's second reign, but this did not necessarily mean that they had gone away.

The contemporary account that asserts their continuing significance most explicitly is the work of an Italian visitor to London in the first half of 1483. Dominic Mancini was a learned and well-connected, although almost certainly non-English speaking, observer. He left England before Richard's coronation and his account, written in the following few months, was thus largely uninfluenced by the unfolding events after the king's accession. But he must have been heavily reliant on what he was told by his informants – certainly for events before his arrival in the country, but also for the explanation of happenings while he was there. His factual errors are relatively easy to spot; more problematic is the status of the opinions he offers. Were these genuinely the views swirling around London and the court at the time (although this does not necessarily mean that they are to be believed), and whose views were they?

Mancini was firm that there was (or had been) a Woodville hegemony in Edward IV's reign: the queen 'attracted to her party many strangers and introduced them to court, so that they alone should manage the public and private business of the crown, surround the king and have bands of retainers, give or sell offices, and finally rule the very king himself'.[15] He was also convinced that it was the queen who had pushed for Clarence's death: 'She concluded that her offspring by the king would never come to the throne, unless the Duke of Clarence were removed.'[16] It has sometimes been argued that this was because Clarence knew that she was not legally the king's wife – the 'pre-contract' argument Richard was to use in June 1483 against the legitimacy of Edward and Elizabeth's firstborn son, the Prince of Wales.[17] But Clarence's previous track record of treason would in itself have been reason enough for the queen's anxieties. In either case, Mancini chose to read the episode as evidence of Richard's alienation from a Woodville-dominated environment and the explanation of his withdrawal from court thereafter.

It is impossible now to gauge Richard's likely reaction to his brother's execution, but his own absence from Edward's court between 1480 and 1482 can more straightforwardly be explained by his leading role in the developing war against Scotland. He had been made lieutenant-general of the army in May 1480 and was to lead the first raid across the border later that year. His status as lieutenant presupposed that the king would take command, but Edward never did and when, after a further year of raiding, the English army mounted its invasion in 1482, Richard was at its head. The army entered Edinburgh unopposed, but then retreated, with very little achieved in those three years beyond the capture of Berwick – the defence costs of which were to prove an anxiety to the royal council thereafter. The major gains were Richard's own. In the parliament of January 1483, by way of reward, he was granted all the royal lands and rights in Cumberland, together with his existing wardenship of the West March, to hold to him and the heirs male of his body. As long as their line lasted, Cumberland was to be a county palatine analogous to the bishopric of Durham. Richard was also to hold on the same basis any land he conquered on the other side of the border.[18] Less tangible, but equally significant, was the assertion of his status as acknowledged lord of the north. For the duration of the campaign he had been the commander of almost all the northern lords and gentry. Many of the latter received their knighthood, or were raised to the status of banneret, at his hand.[19]

Richard was thus riding very high at the beginning of 1483; much higher than Mancini seems to have picked up. Whatever Richard's attitude to the Woodvilles, it is obvious that while Edward lived he had nothing to fear personally from them – nor they from him, although their regional power was very much less than his. Less than two months after parliament rose on 18 February, Edward IV was dead and the world changed.

2

The Protector

On 9 April 1483, Edward IV died at Westminster, leaving the twelve-year-old Prince of Wales as his heir. In the context of a personal monarchy the accession of a child was always deeply problematic. The problems could be – and in the past had been – weathered but they were real and in 1483 there was no established precedent for handling them. Each of the three previous royal minorities had produced a different solution, dictated by circumstances at the time. What Edward IV himself may have wanted is unknown: the codicils he added to his will on his deathbed no longer survive. But in any case a king's wishes in this respect had no legal force: once he was dead, the rule of the kingdom was not in his gift.

In April 1483 immediate authority thus rested *de facto* with the dead king's council at Westminster. The format of the minority government necessarily came under discussion there, and no doubt also informally among the lords and leading household men assembled for the king's exequies. Two of the crucial players in any future scenario were, however, missing from the discussion. The prince's paternal and maternal uncles, Richard, Duke of Gloucester, and Anthony, Earl Rivers, were still making their way slowly towards Westminster: the former travelling down from Yorkshire; the latter, bringing the prince with him, from Ludlow in the Welsh March where the prince's household had been based. In their absence it was agreed that the prince's coronation as Edward V should take place on 4 May, following hard upon his anticipated arrival in the city. This was the easy bit. More contentious was the question of governance. The fullest account of the ensuing disputes comes from the series of additional entries made in the chronicle of Crowland Abbey (Lincolnshire) in 1487. No one has yet managed to identify their author definitively; what can be deduced is that he had been in the service of Edward IV and probably remained in that of Richard III, given what looks at times like eye-witness reportage. The Continuator, as the author of the additional, Yorkist, section is now generally known, was evidently an insider and his commentary on Richard's reign, although sometimes distinctly sour, seems trustworthy.

An adolescent king in some respects posed a more immediate problem than a babe in arms. The minority would be shorter, but the young king's own views and wishes would sooner need to be taken into account – Henry VI had been chafing at the bit before his thirteenth birthday – and Edward V's familial and emotional links were with his maternal kin. In the debates that ensued in April 1483, William, Lord Hastings, was loud in his calls for limitations on Woodville power in the new regime. The late king's household chamberlain, Hastings was the one of Edward IV's circle who had been most clearly at odds with the queen's family in the previous reign and Edward on his deathbed had urged reconciliation between him and the Marquess of Dorset, the queen's eldest son by her first marriage, evidently in vain. Hastings reputedly wanted the Duke of Gloucester to be made regent – an ambiguous title, implying some form of over-arching authority – although that proposal got nowhere, and a consensus seemed to be forming instead around the model adopted during the minority of Richard II: conciliar rule with a designated head of the council, but no appointed regent or Protector. This did nothing to allay Hastings' anxieties, which now focused on the size of the force accompanying Rivers and the prince, and he talked of withdrawing to Calais (where he had been Edward IV's lieutenant) if their numbers were not reduced. It is hard to know how widely such anxieties were shared. The Continuator notes that Hastings' wish to deny the Woodvilles control of the young king was backed by the 'more foresighted' councillors. This is understandable given the implications of *control*, with its suggested manipulation of the boy, and the council had already rejected the idea of a single dominant figure within the minority government.

The queen acquiesced in the reduction of her son's escort. Both Mancini and the Continuator are clear that Hastings' demand for a smaller retinue was not defensive but aggressive, and that he was envisaging the seizure of the prince by force as a first step in denying the prince's maternal uncles and half-brothers any role about his person. He had apparently made this explicit in a letter calling upon Gloucester to bring a large force south with him and seize the prince en route to London, and all the suggestions are that he saw Richard as an ally against the queen's family. Whether Richard needed the prompting is moot. As he journeyed south, he had proposed a rendezvous with the prince and his escort so that they could make their entry into London together. On 29 April, Richard arrived in Northampton, where he had arranged to join forces with Henry Stafford, Duke of Buckingham. The latter had been a marginal figure in the previous reign; born after his father's death in 1455, his marriage was purchased by Edward IV in 1464 and he was shortly afterwards married off to the queen's sister Katherine. Buckingham resented the marriage or, perhaps more to the point, the fact that it brought him no tangible benefits in terms of high office. His only (nominal) role of significance had been acting as High Steward of England at the trial of Clarence in 1478. Now he eagerly hitched his star to Richard's.

That evening, the two dukes hosted an apparently amicable meeting with Rivers and his companions, who had ridden over from Stony Stratford where they had left the prince and his other attendants. At first light the next morning the visitors were roused from their beds and arrested, and the dukes rode together to take possession of the prince and to arrest other key members of Rivers' entourage. The accounts of the Continuator and Mancini differ in several details, but both chose to stress the profound respect with which the two dukes saluted the prince before accusing his arrested companions (one of them Richard Grey, the prince's step-brother) of conspiring against him. The party returned to Northampton and from there on 2 May a letter was sent in the prince's name to the chancellor, Thomas Rotherham, Archbishop of York, ordering him to see to the safe-keeping of the great seal, the Tower and the royal treasure. The coronation of Edward V was postponed.

Richard had engineered a devastatingly effective pre-emptive strike. His account of events, in letters reportedly sent to the royal council and to the Mayor of London, was that he had taken action against a conspiracy that threat-ened not just his own safety but that of the kingdom and of the young king himself: not a coup, then, but a necessary counter-attack. Whether he seriously believed in a Wood-ville conspiracy and whether, if he did, he was right to do so, can now only be a matter of opinion. Certainly Rivers and his kinsmen had been wrong-footed in a way which suggests that they were singularly unprepared to meet opposition. In any case, it was Richard's version of events that had 'won' and which reached a wider audience two days later, on 4 May, when he, Buckingham and the prince entered London. Buckingham was in blue velvet, Richard, an anonymous observer commented, in coarse black cloth.[1] This formal civic entry included an unscheduled four cart-loads of weapons which criers identified as having been captured from the conspirators. Richard was presenting himself, in a literal sense, as the young king's defender and protector, and by 8 May he had taken up the office formally.

Not everyone believed Richard's version of events. Man-cini suggests that Londoners greeted the display of weapons with cynicism. But the Woodvilles and their allies were in disarray – those taken at Stony Stratford had been sent north as prisoners and their supporters in London had scattered after an abortive attempt to rally support – and no one else, at this stage, was in a position to challenge the duke's fait accompli. Some positively welcomed the outcome: Hastings, unsurprisingly, was said to be delighted.[2] The majority view was probably closer to anxious acceptance. No one wanted to open up a contest that could slide into overt violence: those four wagons of weapons had a resonance beyond their immediate message. There were, however, limits to the council's acquiescence. Before his entry into London, Richard had upped the stakes by claiming that the Woodvilles' conspiracy amounted to treason, and he now demanded the death penalty for the captured Rivers and his nephew Richard Grey. The council refused, according to Mancini, on the grounds that any attack on Gloucester before he was Protector could not be considered treason. But the duke's accusation was surely intended to make the same point that he had made to the prince at Stony Stratford: that the Woodville conspiracy had been against the young king, for whose protection he had taken action.

After Richard's recognition as Protector, things seemed to settle down; so much so that the next few weeks disappear almost completely from the Continuator's account. The council was preoccupied with major problems inherited from the previous reign, another reason for not wanting to rock the boat. Months earlier, the European diplomatic situation had been transformed by the Treaty of Arras between France and Burgundy, agreed on 23 December 1482. England, hitherto attempting to juggle relations with both countries, was left out in the cold. Although Edward

IV had backed off from his initial bellicose response, existing tensions between French and English shipping escalated and by the time of his death there was a French fleet in the Channel, preying on English shipping. The parliament that met in January 1483 had granted taxation for defence of the realm, but that was not due to be collected until midsummer. The royal treasury, drained by three years of war against Scotland without taxation revenue, was almost empty and major expenditure was looming – notably for the forthcoming coronation, now rescheduled for 22 June. As the council at Westminster anxiously totted up possible future incomings against immediate outgoings, and scrabbled for new sources of revenue, Richard put his hand into his own pocket to contribute to the costs of the royal household.[3]

During these weeks Richard embarked on a comprehensive dismemberment of Woodville power. Although there had as yet been no formal judicial process against members of the family, their land was treated as forfeit and seized. This was true not only of those arrested at Stony Stratford but of the whole family and their associates, other than the queen's brother Lionel, Bishop of Salisbury. Some of the seizures were authorized under the royal signet, which was by now in Richard's control as Protector. But many were not, and become visible in the record only when the land was regranted or its revenues paid into the Exchequer. In such cases, who had been sent to make the forfeiture is not normally mentioned, but one exception is the seizure of Ightham Mote in Kent, the home of the queen's cousin Richard Haute, one of those arrested at

Stony Stratford. This was carried out by Sir Thomas Wort-
ley, a knight of Edward IV's household, one of those who
had carried the dead king's body to its lying-in-state in
Westminster Abbey and kept vigil over it the night before
its burial at Windsor.[4]

A similar pattern is apparent elsewhere. The Woodville
family's royal offices were now recognized as up for grabs,
as were those of their closest associates, and the recorded
beneficiaries were generally servants of Edward IV rather
than of Richard himself. The duke also turned to his
brother's former servants in his efforts to capture the Woodville family members still at large. Potentially the most
threatening of these was the queen's brother Sir Edward
Woodville, who, shortly before news of the events at Stony
Stratford reached London, had been given authority to
commandeer a fleet to deal with the French threat in the
Channel. Most of his fleet subsequently surrendered, their
Genoese crews having no wish to get drawn into an English quarrel, but Woodville himself escaped with two ships.
He also took with him £10,250 in English gold coin which
he had seized from a carrack in Southampton Water on 14
May as forfeit to the crown.[5] It would be a useful war chest.

In all of this, Richard was keeping to his self-appointed
role as upholder of the good government of his brother;
'good', that is, once purged of the corruption bred by the
queen's family. The servants of Edward IV deployed
against Edward Woodville were apparently willing to support the duke in that enterprise, and, although behind
Richard lay his northern power base, there was at this
stage no sense of a northern takeover. That the immediate

spoils of the Woodvilles' fall also went predominantly to household men of the dead king sent the same message.[6] But in the course of June this apparently harmonious progression towards the young king's coronation was to be blown apart. The steps towards this outcome are well known. How they are to be interpreted is fiercely contested.

Richard's attempts to round up the remaining male Woodvilles and their adherents had so far met with no success. Sir Edward had taken refuge in Brittany. The queen's eldest son, the Marquess of Dorset, was thought to be lurking somewhere on the south coast. The first surviving evidence that Richard's action against the family had moved on to a different level comes on 10 June. On that day he wrote under his own signet to the city of York, appealing for their help against 'the queen, her blood, adherents and affinity, which hath intended and daily doth intend to murder and utterly destroy us and our cousin, the duke of Buckingham, and the old royal blood of this realm . . .'. The next day letters were despatched to the Earl of Northumberland and to Ralph Neville, heir to the Earl of Westmorland, asking them to raise troops in all haste.[7]

That the Woodvilles were conspiring to bring down Richard must surely have been a given. Whatever their intentions might have been in April 1483, by June their only remaining option was to try to dislodge the Protector by force. Richard's response to the threat, echoing and amplifying his accusation against Rivers and others made at the end of April, is equally predictable. What is harder to assess is whether the Woodvilles at this stage really did pose a credible threat to his position. Their motive was indubitable;

the strength of support they could demand uncertain. The duke's letter of the 10th continues: '. . . and, as is now openly known, by their subtle and damnable ways forecasted the same, and also the final destruction and disinheritance of you and all the other inheritors and men of honour, as well of the north parts as other countries that belong [to] us'. Richard was here appealing to his northern heartland, a foretaste of his response to southern rebellion later in the year. The letter, however, seems barely to be about a material threat at all but rather about intention. 'Forecasting' the king's death – casting his horoscope to see when he was due to die – had become a regular element in late-medieval treason accusations on both sides of the Channel. In England it had featured most recently in the trial of Thomas Burdet and Dr John Stacy, which had formed the prelude to the arrest and condemnation of the Duke of Clarence in 1477–8. The felonious subtext was always that this was not just curiosity about *when* the king might die, but a desire that it *should* happen and, by implication, the willingness to deploy occult methods to see that it did. It was a potent smear technique and Richard was here using it as such. He was implicitly reactivating the accusation of treason he had made at the beginning of May, with himself and the old royal blood (a phrase he was to use repeatedly) the destined victims.

No other surviving source gives any indication that these developments were 'openly known'. On the previous day, 9 June, the council had still been fretting about the cost of the coronation and how it was to be met. On the same day Simon Stallworth, in a letter from London to Sir

William Stonor in Oxfordshire, had little that was new to report. The young king was still at the Tower. Richard's duchess, Anne, had arrived in London on the previous Thursday, the 5th; the goods of the Marquess of Dorset were being seized; the queen with her younger son, the Duke of York, and her brother Lionel, Bishop of Salisbury, were still holed up at Westminster.[8] This could hardly be considered business as usual, but it was to be another four days before the mood was to be decisively shattered.

On Friday 13 June, a specially appointed subset of the royal council met in the Tower while the main body met at Westminster as usual; an arrangement made by Richard himself on the previous day. There are various versions of what happened next, and the only consensus is that Richard announced the existence of a conspiracy against him and that the meeting ended with William, Lord Hastings, killed out of hand (murdered in a scuffle or hustled off to immediate execution). A number of the other councillors present – Thomas Rotherham, Archbishop of York (whom Richard had sacked as chancellor back in May), John Morton, Bishop of Ely, and the late king's secretary, Oliver King – were arrested. Later sources, including the London Chronicler, add Thomas, Lord Stanley, to those present and Thomas More (whose informant was probably Morton) offers a vivid little vignette of Stanley being struck over the head when soldiers piled into the room and hiding under the table with blood running down round his ears.[9] Two themes can be picked out of the chroniclers' bewilderment. Tudor writers – although not the immediate contemporaries, Mancini and the Continuator – introduce the accusation of witchcraft (*malefica*) to the story, with Richard revealing his 'withered' arm (presumably an oblique reference to his scoliosis) as evidence of the queen's sorcery against him. Thomas More is the most explicit on this: the statement that he puts into Richard's mouth about those 'that compass and imagine the death of me that am so near of blood unto the king' echoes Richard's own claims in his letter to York and it is likely that it did indeed play a central role in Richard's accusation here too.[10] The sorcery motif was to appear again very shortly afterwards in the attempt to delegitimize Edward's marriage to Elizabeth Woodville, later claimed in the *titulus regius* (the later assertion of Richard's right to the crown) to be the result of sorcery and witchcraft by Elizabeth and her mother Jacquetta, Duchess of Bedford.

The arrest of Thomas Rotherham may not have been surprising. More claimed that at the death of Edward IV the chancellor had handed the great seal to the queen after news had arrived of the events at Stony Stratford, but had then had second thoughts and retrieved it; which would explain his demotion by Richard on 10 May and his treatment now. He remained under a cloud; a few months later Richard ordered the archbishop's tenants to stop withholding their dues, something which could indicate unilateral action on the tenants' part, but more probably implies the previous seizure of the archbishop's properties (also the fate that befell John Morton).[11] By contrast, everyone, both at the time and now, seems to have been baffled by the attack on Hastings, hitherto Richard's enthusiastic supporter. The Continuator intensifies the sense of shock by telescoping recent events in his account, so that Hastings' delight in Richard's appointment as Protector – 'bursting with joy over this new world' – is followed in 'a very few days' by his denunciation and death. Mancini moralizes: 'Thus fell Hastings, killed not by those enemies he had always feared, but by a friend he had never doubted. But whom will insane lust for power spare . . . ?'[12] Given Hastings' loyalty to Edward IV and, presumably, to his heirs there are really only two viable explanations: either he already feared that Richard's ultimate intention was to take the throne for himself and had made it clear that he would not acquiesce; or Richard assumed that this would be the case and went for (another) pre-emptive strike.

The Continuator seems to regard the episode as a cynical move *pour encourager les autres*: 'these two dukes [Gloucester and Buckingham] thereafter did whatever they wanted.' Mancini's response is more nuanced, at least as far as Richard's ultimate intentions are concerned. He follows his account of initial panic in the city, calmed by the duke's assurance that a dangerous plot had been safely quashed, with a caveat. Although it was beginning to dawn on people that Richard coveted the crown 'yet there remained some hope . . . inasmuch as he still professed to do all these things as an avenger of treason and old wrongs'.[13] This paralysing desire to go on hoping for the best is demonstrated by what happened next. At some point over the next two days, Richard persuaded the remaining council members that the presence of the Duke of York would be needed at his brother's coronation, still scheduled for 22 June. On Monday the 16th, members of the council – headed by the Archbishop of Canterbury and respected Yorkist stal-wart Cardinal Thomas Bourchier; the new chancellor John Russell, Bishop of Lincoln; and 'many Lords Temporal' – waited on the dowager queen at Westminster and persuaded her to hand over her younger son, Prince Richard.

Although this was achieved without overt force, all parties concerned must have been acutely conscious of the threat of violence being unleashed. The Continuator talks of a 'great crowd, with swords and clubs' coming by river to the abbey, and terrorizing Cardinal Bourchier into taking the lead in persuading the queen.[14] What observers in London could not yet know was that the letters for troops despatched by the Protector on the 10th and 11th had already had their effect. The letter to York had arrived on the 15th and by the following day the Earl of Northumberland was raising men in Yorkshire's East Riding. The troops assembled under the earl and Richard Ratcliff, one of the Protector's retainers, at Pontefract, where the imprisoned Rivers, Richard Grey and Thomas Vaughan (Edward IV's treasurer of the chamber) were executed, and then the army headed south.

In London, the handing over of Prince Richard on the 16th was followed later on the same day by the postponement of the coronation until 9 November. The cancellation of the parliament planned for 25 June, for which writs had gone out on the 13th, soon followed. The writing was now on the wall, and examples begin to occur of official documents being dated by year of grace rather than, as usual, the king's regnal year. In London the response was one of confusion and anxiety. 'With us is much trouble, and every man doubts other,' wrote Simon Stallworth to William Stonor on 21 June. 'I hold you happy that you are out of the press.' Twenty thousand men of Richard and Buckingham were expected imminently, 'to what intent I know not but to keep the peace'. Edward IV's mistress Jane Shore was in prison: 'what shall happen [to] her I know not'. He added a postscript: 'All my lord chamberlain's [Hastings'] men become my lord of Buckingham's men.'[15]

Henry Stafford, Duke of Buckingham, had grabbed with both hands the possibilities offered by backing Richard. Contemporary chroniclers saw him as Richard's alter ego, talking about 'these dukes' almost as if they were one. He had been the major departure from Richard's hitherto rather cautious reshaping of the Yorkist establishment. In a breath-taking series of grants under the signet that began on 15 May, Buckingham was made constable and steward of all the royal lands in the counties of Shropshire, Hereford, Somerset, Dorset and Wiltshire, with power of array (the authority to raise troops for the king). He received the same offices throughout North and South Wales, where he was also made chief justice and chamberlain, and in the Marches. All of that was to be his for life. He was also, but only during the protectorate, given the right to appoint to all crown offices in Wales, including sheriffs and escheators. He need render no accounts, save as chief justice and chamberlain, for which offices he was granted 1,000 marks (just over £666) for his expenses.[16] It was, on the face of it, an explicit and total transfer of regional authority into one pair of hands. There was one qualification. Buckingham would acquire the offices only as they fell empty. But such a powerful reversionary interest might in practice have proved hard to withstand, even had not the collapse of the Woodville interest already rendered many of the offices effectively vacant. The duke could look forward to control of Wales and a large stake in the West Country for his lifetime.

Now he was also to be the beneficiary of Hastings' fall. The north Midlands had been another area of Stafford interest from which the duke had been excluded by Edward IV, and one of Richard's first grants as king would give all Hastings' duchy of Lancaster offices in the region to the duke.[17] The migration of Hastings' men towards him, reported in June, suggests that such a grant was anticipated, had probably even been made although no formal record of it survives. Central government was by now slowing to a halt. In the signet office the last document to be issued was dated 13 June. That may owe something to the arrest of Edward IV's secretary, Oliver King, that day, but the last issued under the great seal where Russell remained in office, was only two days later. It was evidently assumed that grants under the seal of Edward V would shortly become worthless.

During that week Richard put off his mourning and often rode through the city – in purple raiment, the royal colour – showing himself to the people to receive their applause; although Mancini, probably in this case an eyewitness, suggests that the move misfired and that people refused to respond. On 22 June any remaining uncertainty about what was happening was finally dispelled when the preacher at St Paul's Cross, the heart of London's information network, publicized the duke's title to the throne in the presence of a huge audience reputedly including both Richard and Buckingham. The London Chronicler and Mancini both believed that the version preached on that occasion was that Edward IV himself was illegitimate, which necessarily barred his children from inheriting the throne.[18] This was not well received by its audience, nor, one would imagine, by the duke's mother had she ever got to hear of it, and was hastily dropped from subsequent versions of Richard's claim.

Over the next few days there seems to have been an exercise in damage limitation. Buckingham visited the Lords (according to Mancini) and the mayor and citizens of London (according to the London Chronicler), urging their support for the duke's claim to the throne, this time emphasizing the illegitimacy of Edward's children, rather than of the king himself. On 26 June, Richard was petitioned to take the throne. The text survives only on the parliament roll of January 1484, some six months after the coronation, and is there described as a petition of the three estates 'presented and actually delivered' to the king in June 'in the name of the three estates of this realm of England', which he 'for the public weal and tranquillity of this land, benignly accepted'. Quite who constituted the three estates in this context is left unstated, except that there were a lot of them.[19] It has sometimes been suggested that they were the men who had arrived for the parliament meeting planned for the previous day before news of its cancellation reached them; but it could have just as well been a specially constructed gathering.

The petition (the *titulus regius*), the 'official' version of

Richard's claim, rehearses that Edward, before his marriage to Elizabeth Woodville, had been pre-contracted to another woman, Eleanor, daughter of the Earl of Shrewsbury and the widow of Thomas Butler of Sudeley, Gloucestershire. To strengthen the case, it also casts aspersions on the king's 'secret' marriage to Elizabeth Woodville, contrary to 'the laudable custom of the church of England'. The claim made earlier that Edward himself might be a bastard is only lightly touched upon, in the comment that because Richard had been born in England (unlike his three elder brothers, although this is only spelled out in the case of the Duke of Clarence, who had been born in Ireland) it was possible to have more certain knowledge of his birth and parentage. Clarence's son, the young Earl of Warwick, was ruled out by his father's attainder.

The petition goes well beyond what Richard had been claiming in his recorded statements hitherto. The shared ground was the toxic effect of the Woodville marriage, by which 'the order of all politic rule was perverted'. The bigamous marriage of Edward IV is a new component. Richard's earlier emphasis had been, rather, on the need to rescue the prince from the malign influence of his mother's family. The *titulus regius*, however, was also now all but explicitly critical of Edward IV himself. Those who had the rule of the land – i.e. the late king and his associates – 'delighting in adulation and flattery and led by sensuality and concupiscence, followed the counsel of insolent, vicious people of inordinate avarice'.[20] Accusations of sexual misbehaviour were to become the leitmotif of Richard's proclamations against his opponents, most of whom were to be found among Edwardian loyalists. Perhaps this *was* in the end how Richard had come to see his brother and his reign. Piling all the blame on the Woodvilles, as he had done earlier, did not necessarily preclude the possibility of disillusionment with his brother as well.

Contemporary commentators remained unpersuaded. The Crowland Continuator characterized the petition as sedition and infamy.[21] Mancini and the London Chronicler seem to ignore it altogether, suggesting that Richard's title was accepted out of fear rather than conviction. Doubt was more obliquely registered by John, Lord Dynham, the commander of Calais. In an undated letter, addressed to Richard as Protector, Dynham, with studied artlessness, enquired what was to be done about the oath that he and the Calais garrison had taken to the young Edward V upon the death of his father. Richard's answer was that people in many parts of England as well as Calais had taken that oath

> being then ignorant of the very sure and true title which our sovereign lord that now is, king Richard the third, hath and had the same time to the Crown of England. That oath notwithstanding, now every true Englishman is bound upon knowledge had of the said very true title to depart from the first oath so ignorantly given to him whom it appertained not and thereupon to make his oath of new . . .

That true title, Richard's letter continued, was set out in the bill of 26 June, a copy of which was to be sent to Calais. Once it had been read, 'all manner of persons' were to take their oath to Richard as their sovereign lord 'as the lords spiritual and temporal and many other noble men in great number being in England freely and of good heart have done for their part'.[22]

June 26th marked the formal beginning of Richard's reign. The event was carefully staged. The petition was presented to him at Baynard's Castle, the London base of the dukes of York. In a ceremony modelled on the accession of Edward IV in 1461, he was then escorted in procession to Westminster Hall, where, now vested in royal robes, he took his seat on the marble chair in the Court of King's Bench and addressed the assembled judges, commanding them to administer his law justly and duly, and without delay or favour. As a symbol of his stated intention to pardon all offences against him, the Woodville associate Sir John Fogge, who had prudently taken refuge in sanctuary, was fetched out and brought to Richard, who clasped him warmly by the hand. The king then entered the abbey, where the *Te Deum* was sung; the procession then re-formed and returned to London. He was now by the grace of God King of England.

3
By the Grace of God, King

Richard was crowned King of England on Sunday 6 July
1483. The coronation was designed to be, and indeed
appeared, a triumphantly Yorkist occasion. The procession from Westminster Hall into the abbey was a roll-call
of the English peerage. The young Earl of Essex carried the
spurs; the new Earl of Nottingham, William Berkeley,
Saint Edward's staff; the Earl of Northumberland, Cur-
tana, one of the four ceremonial swords; Thomas, Lord
Stanley, the constable's mace, deputizing for the Duke of
Buckingham, who, as Lord Chamberlain, was overseeing
the whole show. Francis, Viscount Lovell, Richard's friend
from their early days in the household of the Earl of Warwick, carried the third sword and the Earl of Kent the
second. Richard's brother-in-law the Duke of Suffolk carried the sceptre and his son the Earl of Lincoln the orb.
The newly ennobled Earl of Surrey, Thomas Howard, carried the sword of state and his father John, now Duke of
Norfolk, the crown itself. Queen Anne was preceded by
the Earl of Huntingdon bearing her sceptre, Lord Lisle her
ivory rod and the Earl of Wiltshire her crown. In total
twelve dukes and earls attended, twenty-three viscounts
and barons and around eighty-five knights, not counting

those newly made Knights of the Bath as a prelude to the coronation.[1]

Three of the noble participants – Nottingham, Norfolk and Surrey – had been direct beneficiaries of Richard's seizure of power the previous month. All had been potential claimants to the lands of the Mowbray dukes of Norfolk at the death of the last duke in January 1476, leaving as his heir a daughter, Anne. In January 1478, Edward IV had married her off to his second son, Richard. The child bride had died four years later, at which point the Mowbray inheritance should have passed to the heirs general: William Berkeley and John Howard. But Edward hung on to it. Berkeley had earlier waived his right to inherit in return for the cancellation of his (massive) debts to the crown. Howard had to make do with an agreement that Prince Richard would only have a life interest in the land – but as the boy was then only nine and Howard was in his fifties this was shabby treatment of a man who had hitherto been a loyal workhorse of the regime. On his accession, Richard III had moved quickly to address the injustice: John Howard was created Duke of Norfolk on 28 June (with Berkeley slipstreaming behind him to receive an earldom) and was to remain the king's devoted ally thereafter.[2]

There were of course absentees from the coronation. Earl Rivers, along with Lord Richard Grey and Thomas Vaughan, had been executed at Pontefract the day before Richard claimed the throne for himself. None of the surviving Woodville clan was there either – Elizabeth and her daughters still remained in sanctuary – and nor were some of their former associates: none of the Kentish Haute family, for instance, already targeted during the protectorate, and no Sir John Fogge, in spite of the king's grand gesture in pardoning him on the day of his accession. Richard must still have been expecting trouble from that quarter, but on the face of it the remaining Yorkist establishment had embraced him as their king. Richard's belief that his brother's men *had* accepted his accession is suggested by his continuing readiness to leave office-holders largely undisturbed. Apart from the clearing-out of Woodville associates during the protectorate, he made relatively few changes to local power networks, including the commissions of the peace. The offices that did fall vacant were often granted to former servants of Edward IV; there were at this stage limited pickings for Richard's northern retainers and no expectation that they would move south to fill any gaps. In this respect, at least, his self-identification with the continuity of his brother's regime still held true. But if Richard did indeed believe that he had been accepted by Edward IV's servants, he would soon be proved wrong. Events had moved so quickly between late June and early July that there had been no time for concerted opposition to take shape, even had the collective paralysis at the centre allowed it.

Richard did not remain long in London after his coronation. It was important for a new king to see and be seen and on 19 July he was heading westwards. From Windsor his progress took him initially through Reading to Oxford (where he sat through two academic disputations), Woodstock, Gloucester, Tewkesbury, where his brother the

Duke of Clarence was buried, and Worcester, before turning back to Warwick and then beginning to head north.[3] A king's first entry into a city was always a lavish occasion, characterized by civic pageantry and gift-giving: a ceremonial purse or gold cup full of gold coins was the customary offering. The king might respond with some mark of favour, and Richard's progress can be tracked by the trail of his grants to towns and religious houses en route. He also made a point of refusing the cash gifts, saying that he would rather have men's hearts than their money. Master Thomas Langton, a former chaplain and councillor of Edward IV, who was in Richard's company and soon to be the new Bishop of St David's, reported breathlessly that the king 'contents the people where he goes best that ever did prince'.[4]

Alongside all the acclamation, disaffection was beginning to surface. The king had no doubt expected as much. On 16 July he had given John Howard, the new Duke of Norfolk, sole power of array in the counties of Norfolk, Suffolk, Essex, Hertford, Middlesex, Kent, Sussex, Surrey, Berkshire, Buckingham, Bedford, Cambridge and Huntingdon. Howard had set off on the progress with the king, but turned back to London a few days later, to keep an eye on events in the capital. On 29 July, the king wrote to the chancellor, the Bishop of Lincoln, John Russell, ordering the appointment of a judicial commission to try unnamed men arrested for an 'enterprise'. This was almost certainly the attempt to rescue Edward IV's sons from the Tower recorded by the Tudor antiquary John Stow, who had access to records of legal proceedings now lost. Four men were executed for their part in the plot, one of them a groom of the stirrup of Edward IV, whose involvement hints at input from the former royal household and probably from Sir John Cheyne, the former master of horse. According to the contemporary French chronicler Thomas Basin, fifty Londoners had been involved but the city failed to follow their lead. There were also, according to the Crowland Continuator, attempts to spring Edward IV's daughters from sanctuary and spirit them away to the continent – which Richard countered by putting an armed guard around Westminster under the command of one of his esquires of the body, John Nesfield.[5]

It is clear that these early conspirators were still thinking in terms of the rescue and restoration of Edward V and his siblings, and it is this that provides the most likely context for the death of the princes. The pattern is familiar from previous depositions: the deposed ruler, Edward II or Richard II, would remain alive until a significant rising in his favour demonstrated that he was still a threat to the current regime. Henry VI broke the pattern only because at his capture in 1465 he had a son beyond Edward IV's reach who could have replaced him as a focus for opposition. Only once that son had been killed at Tewkesbury was Henry put to death in the Tower. That Richard was responsible for the death of his nephews was evidently taken for granted at the time and is still much the most likely scenario. Mancini, who left England around the time of Richard's coronation, tells of men bursting into tears when Prince Edward was mentioned: 'already there was a suspicion that he had been done away with.'[6] If this was indeed the case – and it has, of course, been furiously disputed – it marked a departure from earlier precedent in that there was no funeral to confirm the fact of their death; but it is not difficult to imagine why that might have been. The funeral of two children would have been, to put it in modern terms, a public relations disaster. There is at least no doubt that contemporaries thought that they were dead, and acted accordingly. It is inconceivable that the predominantly Yorkist rebels against Richard III would have backed Henry Tudor, in most people's eyes an exiled nonentity with no claim to the throne, as their candidate for king if they had thought that Edward's sons were still available.

Clarence's son, Edward, Earl of Warwick, *was* still available but seems not to have been considered as a claimant. In the *titulus regius* presented on 26 June, Warwick had been firmly ruled out due to the attainder of his father, but attainders could be, and frequently were, reversed. Edward IV himself had been attainted, as Earl of March, in the parliament of 1459 and it had not stopped him becoming king in 1461. It was more to the point that Warwick was a child in Richard's keeping. It is also possible that he was mentally retarded, although the suggestion seems to rest only on a later remark by the Tudor chronicler Edward Hall that the boy couldn't tell a goose from a capon.[7] Henry Tudor, by contrast, was in his late twenties and a free agent. Although an exile in Brittany with his uncle Jasper, in the summer of 1483 his mother Margaret Beaufort was in a position to push him firmly into the picture. She had been active before this in trying to secure her son's recognition as Earl of Richmond: the earldom of his father Edmund, the half-brother of Henry VI. Both Edward IV and Richard III had been prepared to listen to her but had remained unpersuaded and the negotiations had so far come to nothing.[8] Margaret now saw the gathering opposition to Richard as her opportunity to take a different route. The men arrested in July for attempting to rescue the princes had also been accused of communicating with Jasper and Henry Tudor in Brittany. The conspirators' intention was presumably not at this stage to make Henry himself king, but from Margaret's perspective Beaufort/Tudor support for the restoration of Edward V could have brought the desired reward: Henry's restoration to his father's lands and title, and presumably also a significant role within the restored Edwardian polity for him and his family.

These two early conspiracies in London, at least as reported, sound ad hoc and amateurish. Neither threatened to bring down the new regime by force. The first apparently relied on inciting a popular rising in support of the imprisoned children, which then failed to materialize. The second was no more than a rescue bid. There were, however, more powerful forces massing in the background, news of which had begun to reach the king. On 13 August, while Richard took a break from his travels at Warwick, the land of John Welles, explicitly identified as the king's *rebel* (the word is significant), was put into the keeping of John, Lord Scrope of Bolton (Yorkshire).[9] Welles was Margaret Beaufort's half-brother. He had also been a prominent member of Edward IV's household, one of the bearers of the king's coffin four months earlier. His involvement is testimony to the alliance now being forged between the Beaufort and Woodville interests, with, at its heart (although this was not yet made explicit), a proposed marriage between Henry Tudor and Edward IV's eldest daughter, Elizabeth. Four days after the seizure of Welles's land, Richard ordered 2,000 Welsh bills (halberds) to be sent to him in haste. The threat was evidently now one that might require a military response. By 28 August, when Richard had reached Ponte-fract on his journey north, his suspicions were becoming both more acute and more wide-ranging. His 'dearest kins-man', Henry, Duke of Buckingham, was appointed to head a judicial commission of *oyer et terminer* (to hear and to determine) to investigate and judge treasons and felonies in London, Surrey, Sussex, Kent, Middlesex, Oxfordshire, Berkshire, Essex and Hertfordshire: a list of counties that partly paralleled Norfolk's commission of array but which was narrower and more accurately reflects those areas that were to be among the centres of overt rebellion the following October. For over month, however, no more is heard of opposition or of the king's response to it. Rich-ard was, it seems, otherwise occupied. On 29 August, the feast of the Decollation (beheading) of the Baptist, he arrived in York, where he was to stay for just over three weeks: the longest period he had spent anywhere since his coronation.

York was, and was intended to be, the climax of the king's celebratory progress. The city, urged by the king's secretary, John Kendal, a York man himself, to put on an elaborate 'entry' to impress the southerners in the royal retinue, surely rose to the occasion, although details of the ceremonial do not survive.[10] There was to be another, even more spectacular occasion during the royal visit, this time stage-managed by the royal household rather than by the city: the investiture of Richard's son Edward as Prince of Wales. This seems to have been a last-minute decision. An urgent request for the necessary trappings had gone off to the keeper of the wardrobe on 31 August and the investiture itself took place, following Mass in the Minster, in the archbishop's palace on 8 September, the feast of the Nativity of the Virgin. The lavishness of the occasion was later to give rise to the belief that Richard had celebrated a second coronation in York, which was not literally the case – although Richard surely *was* celebrating his own elevation before an audience of his northern allies. The investiture was followed by the king and queen, crowned, making a ceremonial progress through the streets of the city.

All these celebrations did not come cheap. Three days after the investiture the king borrowed £100 in ready money from the Abbot of Furness.[11] On Edward IV's death the cupboard had been almost bare, with little cash in the Treasury. But the mood of the progress, certainly in York, does not seem to have been one of anxious penny-pinching. Langton's letter cited earlier was written in York and after praising the king ('God hath sent him to us for the weal of us all') and his reception by the people, he cautiously shifted into Latin. The text here is barely legible but has been deciphered as a comment on the increasing sensual indulgence of the court.[12] Richard was evidently enjoying being king: the pomp, the adulation, the chance to be open-handed (which on this progress he clearly was), the sheer luxury of it all. The major chronicler of the reign, the Continuator, was later to pick up the same tendency with evident disapproval.

Perhaps this meant that Richard took his eye off the ball for a time. It was not until 20 September that the court left York and turned back south again. The commission of *oyer et terminer* issued at the end of August had been the last explicit indication of unrest. Records of the proceedings of such commissions hardly ever now survive, but there is no sign of fallout from it in the shape of forfeitures of land or arrests. By the time he left York, however, Richard must have been aware of gathering opposition. On 22 September the king ordered the seizure of the temporalities of Lionel Woodville's bishopric of Salisbury. The court then lingered in Pontefract for a further two and a half weeks, which perhaps suggests that the king wanted to stay within easy recruiting distance of his northern retinue until the situation clarified. On 9 October he finally began to move south. He was at Gainsborough, the Lincolnshire home of his knight of the body Thomas Burgh, on Friday 10th and at Lincoln the next day. It was there that for the first time he went public on the defection of the Duke of Buckingham, ordering a general mobilization of forces against the duke, 'who traitorously is turned against us'. Both the Continuator and Polydore Vergil believed that Richard had dissembled his knowledge (provided by an informer) until he had had time to make his preparations, and it is clear from Richard's letter to his chancellor John Russell the following day, asking for the great seal to be sent to him, that they had already been in communication about the subject. But the savagery of Richard's postscript, scribbled in his own hand round the edge of that letter, reveals that his anger at the betrayal was still raw. Buckingham was there characterized, famously, as 'him that had best cause to be true . . . the most untrue creature living'.[13]

Faced by rebellion, money again became a pressing issue. At Lincoln the sheriff of the county, Thomas Knight, supplied 50 marks to the king 'for the great cost which he must bear in subduing the Duke of Buckingham'.[14] By this time, rebellion had already broken out in Kent. Word of it had reached London on 10 October and John Howard sent troops into the county to deal with it and set about organizing the defence of the city. But it must have been evident that unrest was not going to be confined to the eastern side of the country and the royal army was ordered to assemble in the Midlands, at Leicester. By the time it had done so, on 20–21 October, rebels had declared themselves further to the west and south. Centres of opposition later named in the parliamentary Act of Attainder were Buckingham's castle at Brecon, and Newbury, Salisbury and Exeter, although this geographical bundling-up of the rebels obscures some significant areas of unrest elsewhere, notably Southampton, where the city itself was drawn into the rising and the mayor was later attainted for his part in it. As events unfolded it became clear that this was no longer only a Woodville/Stafford/Tudor enterprise, but opposition from within the heart of Edward IV's household and affinity. Many of its identifiable protagonists were men whose loyalty Richard had assumed he could take for granted, who had attended his coronation and whom he had hitherto retained in local office; men such as George Brown, John Guildford, Giles Daubeney and John Cheyne.[15]

In the end the rebellion collapsed without ever coming to battle. There were skirmishes in Kent, including an affray in the fair at Gravesend, and reports of groups of rebels moving about the country – a servant of the Sheriff of Cornwall walked into a band of them in the Wiltshire town of Warminster and had the documents he was carrying stolen.[16] But the various components never cohered. By the time the royal army reached Salisbury, Buckingham's own forces had dissolved, and the duke himself had been captured. He was executed in Salisbury marketplace on 2 November, All Souls' Day, after Richard had refused a meeting with him. From there the royal army headed into the West Country, a region not identified as a possible site of unrest earlier in the year, but where trouble had flared up in Exeter and further west. By now, however, any opposition was effectively over.[17] The last identifiable act of rebellion was the proclamation of Henry Tudor at Bodmin on 3 November – a futile gesture because, although Tudor had taken ship for England, he did not make the mistake of landing. The circuit the king made through Dorset, Devon and Somerset was essentially a mopping-up exercise, reaching its climax in the execution of a small group of western rebels at Exeter before the king turned back towards London.

For the Continuator, as in the subsequent parliamentary Act of Attainder, it was Buckingham who was the leading figure in the rising, and the episode continues to be known as *Buckingham's* rebellion. He was also, according to the chronicler, the primary cause of its failure. Richard's early discovery of Buckingham's involvement meant that the duke could be boxed into the southern Welsh Marches. As Buckingham advanced from Brecon, his vengeful former employees the Vaughans of Tretower sacked the castle at his back and blocked the route out of Wales. In torrential rain, Humphrey Stafford of Grafton and his brother Thomas were also able to block the Severn crossings against the duke.[18] Finding himself holed up at Weobley, on the Leominster road, Buckingham abandoned the enterprise and fled in disguise. Significantly, he seems to have fled northwards and another contributory factor in the rebellion's failure may thus be the equivocal role played by Lord Stanley and his son George, Lord Strange. On 18 October, as Richard headed for the muster at Leicester, Strange's secretary wrote to his kinsman Sir Robert Plumpton reporting that both Richard and Buckingham were recruiting in the north-west. He added that Strange would be setting out on the following Monday, the 20th, with ten thousand men, 'whither, we cannot say'.[19]

Lord Stanley was the husband of Margaret Beaufort, whose own wish for Richard's removal is undoubted. But he was a notoriously canny operator, with a knack for sitting on the sidelines until he could be sure of ending up on the right side. He managed it again this time. It must have been on the cards that he would have thrown his forces behind the rebels. Tudor was, after all, his stepson. Had he done so, his joining with Buckingham could have opened a front of rebellion right up the west side of the country, creating a pincer movement with the rising of Edwardian servants across the south and south-west. However, if this had indeed been the plan it may have foundered not so much on Buckingham's being kettled west of the Severn as on hostility among the former servants of Edward IV in Wales and the Marches to the duke's potentially complete takeover of local office. None of them appears to have backed the rising. Their loyalties were to be very different in 1485.

Buckingham's role before and after Richard's accession poses one of the most intractable questions raised by these months. His grants from the new regime had been unparalleled. Part of the first tranche made under the protectorate was only to have been activated on the deaths of the current holders, but much of it was intended to take immediate effect. All of it was confirmed immediately after Richard's accession. So was the promised grant of all the duchy of Lancaster offices in the north Midlands formerly held by Hastings. Potentially far more significant even than this was the king's apparent willingness to dismember the duchy of Lancaster on the duke's behalf. An entry in the signet archive records a grant made under Richard's signet and sign manual at Greenwich on 13 July 1483, a week after the coronation, which transferred to the duke, for his 'true, laudable and faithful service', the share of the great Bohun inheritance formerly held by the house of Lancaster, and taken over by Edward IV on his accession. The inheritance had been divided in the early fifteenth century between Henry V and Anne Stafford, Buckingham's great-grandmother, and the duke now claimed Lancaster's share on the strength of Henry VI's death without surviving heirs. Although the grant would require parliamentary ratification, the duke was authorized to enter the land at once and enjoy its revenues and the disposal of office within it. Had it been confirmed, the gift would have stripped forty manors and other assets – itemized in careful detail in an appendix to the grant – from the royal estate.[20]

Why Buckingham was thought to deserve this level of reward is inexplicable. Later writers seem to have regarded him as something of a lightweight, as, apparently, did Edward IV, who allowed him no significant role. It is striking, however, that Mancini and the Continuator talk of him as the Duke of Gloucester's equal in the events of spring 1483, at least initially. The phrase 'these two dukes' recurs. Were the great rewards, which began almost immediately once Richard as Protector had the power to make them, intended to be consolation for the fact that only one man could wear the crown? Even more perplexing is Buckingham's apparent readiness to then gamble his gains away in rebellion, especially as there are no signs that his earlier power grab was being clawed back and it is unlikely that he could have hoped for *more* from another regime. The Continuator simply claims that the duke repented what had been done, although this too seems unlikely. A more cynical (but also much more probable) explanation is that, as opposition to Richard gathered, Buckingham began seeing himself as a possible replacement. The duke could, after all, claim royal descent – which was to bring his son to the block in 1521. This was to be the line taken by Thomas More, who gives the credit for 'turning' Buckingham to

John Morton, Bishop of Ely, placed in the duke's custody after his arrest on 13 June. His account shows the bishop playing on exactly this idea: that Buckingham would prove a better, more deserving ruler than the current incumbent.[21] It was evidently music to the duke's ears.

Exactly what was going on in Buckingham's circle, and what his own contribution to the rising was, is unclear. The 1484 Act of Attainder passed against the rebels was to assign only three rebels to the Brecon sector, other than the duke and the bishop: a Norfolk knight (William Knyvet), a London merchant (John Rushe) and Thomas Nandyke, 'necromancer' (who was to pop up again in unrest in the east of England in the following year). Necromancy meant sorcery and the use of the word here was analogous to the accusations made in Richard's earlier attacks on his enemies. But quite what Nandyke – a Cambridge Master of Arts with an interest in medicine and astronomy – might have contributed to the conspiracy went unrecorded.[22]

The rebellion had failed. But it left behind a poisonous legacy. Richard's claim to the throne had been denied the divine sanction represented by victory in battle, and for the rest of his reign he seems to have been hankering for the chance to obtain it. He dragged his feet over negotiating a truce with Scotland, probably in part because he saw that very much as 'his' war. When in 1484 a French attack on Calais was rumoured and the Cinque Ports were ordered to prepare for resistance, Richard was clearly up for it. He self-identified as 'that prince which for the defence of his realm and all the possessions of the crown of England is disposed to employ his own royal person as far as ever any king hath done'.[23] Most tellingly, when Henry Tudor finally invaded in 1485, Richard is said to have rejoiced at the news.

The disintegration of the rising also denied him the security of dealing conclusively with his enemies – or, indeed, of being able to identify all of them with certainty. Many of the rebels, especially those in the south-west, had been able to escape into exile in Brittany and the close of the year saw heavy royal expenditure on sea defences off the west coast.[24] Other rebels went to ground in England. Relatively few had been captured and perhaps no more than ten were executed, among them Sir Thomas St Leger, the widower of Richard's sister the dowager duchess of Exeter. St Leger was firmly within the Woodville camp. His daughter by the duchess had been allowed to inherit the duchy and had been given in marriage to the son of Thomas Grey, Marquess of Dorset, Queen Elizabeth's son by her first marriage. Richard had been expecting opposition from this grouping, whose power he had been unpicking from the very outset of the reign. Most of them, including Elizabeth Woodville herself, had suffered forfeiture before the rebellion broke, although without formal judicial process.

What the king had demonstrably not expected was the involvement of so many other members of his brother's establishment: men whom in many cases he had retained in their household and local offices after his accession. His initial sales pitch to them in April had been in effect the preservation of his brother's government minus the Woodvilles, and he had apparently found no difficulty about using them at that stage in the steps taken against the family.

Although by the end of June that self-representation must have been wearing rather thin, given that his public criticism was now increasingly directed at Edward himself, he seems to have been genuinely shocked by the extent of the backlash in October. A sense of the panic evoked by the scale of the disaster is reflected in Richard's order to seize the land of *all* the gentry and household men in Wiltshire, rather than just named rebels.[25]

The motives of the rebels themselves were, of course, various. Some had personal axes to grind: the fear that Richard's associates – the new ingredient in the mix – might in time come to threaten their own position, even if they had not already done so. But many for whom there is no other obvious motive must surely have been driven simply by the sense that what Richard had done in deposing his nephew was unacceptable. Loyal servants of Edward IV who had shown themselves perfectly willing to cut back the power of the Woodvilles evidently drew the line at that. It may be that Hastings had been the first to see where events were heading, but from that point realization would have dawned swiftly. If, back in August, Richard had indeed seen the princes' death as a way of cutting the ground from under the feet of emerging rebels, he was now reaping the whirlwind. It was to be the scale of the rebellion, rather than any initial opposition to his accession, that drove the king to retreat into the security of his own, predominantly northern, connection. The seizure of the rebels' land and office was already well under way as the king travelled through the south-west in November. The speed of his response meant that corners were cut.

Men commissioned to seize the land of rebels – initially a defensive move as much as a penal one – generally seem to have been left to identify the land involved for themselves. In these circumstances mistakes were made: land held in a wife's right was exempt from forfeiture but was sometimes swept up into the resulting royal grant. On occasion, royal allies might obtain possession of land held by rebels without the necessary legal process. Sir Ralph Ashton was apparently one such beneficiary of forfeitures in Kent.[26] When the Act of Attainder formalizing the forfeitures was passed in the parliament of January 1484, it included the precaution of retrospectively legitimating grants that had been made already without formal inquiry.

From the king's perspective, the rapid transfer of land and office in rebel areas into the hands of his loyal supporters was a political necessity. The beneficiaries were predominantly the members of Richard's northern connection who now, often for the first time, were reaping a lavish reward from his accession. In moving south and assuming possession of their new roles, they tended to take with them their associates to share the bonanza. The result, according to the Continuator, was a northern invasion of the south, with which Richard's regime has been associated ever since.

4
Picking Up the Pieces

The failure of Buckingham's rebellion brought Richard no security. There was now an acknowledged (and persuasive) rival for the crown in the shape of Henry Tudor, who was safely back in Brittany after his aborted attempt to land in the south-west. In Rennes Cathedral on Christmas morning 1483, he swore on the sacrament that, were he to take the throne, he would marry Edward IV's daughter Elizabeth. This was the cue for his followers to kneel and formally do him homage as their king. If in the previous October Yorkist support for him had been *faute de mieux*, given his Lancastrian pedigree and lack of any real title to the throne, it would in future be much more enthusiastic and Richard knew it. For the moment, though, Richard had a breathing space. His own Christmas was given over to the celebration of his triumph – the Continuator rather sniffily 'passes over' the extravagance of the occasion – and then came the meeting of parliament at Westminster on 23 January, postponed from 9 November. From the king's perspective it had two main items of business. One was the formal assertion of his title, in the shape of the petition presented to him in June (the *titulus regius*). The other was the condemnation of his opponents.

The main Act of Attainder lists ninety-eight men, the largest number ever attainted at one time. Even then it was far from a complete list of those implicated. A separate act dealt with the particular position of Margaret Beaufort, who escaped attainder for the sake of her husband Lord Stanley's 'good and faithful service', but was stripped of her own titles, property and income. The three bishops involved in the rebellion (Piers Courtenay of Exeter had joined Lionel Woodville and John Morton in opposition) also needed separate attention. Although, as their Act of Attainder stated, they deserved to lose their life, land and goods, because the king 'prefers mercy and pity to rigour', they were stripped only of all their temporal and feudal possessions.[1] Impressive as the length of the list is, it is far from a complete tally of those known to have been involved. A handful of those implicated managed to buy themselves off during the life of the parliament with grants of land to the king or his allies. William Knyvet, who had been Buckingham's companion at Brecon, later claimed to have paid 700 marks to the king, 100 marks to the queen and handed over four of his manors to the king and other land to Sir James Tyrell, a man of known influence about the king.[2] The names of numerous others who escaped attainder – but who none the less suffered forfeiture – can be found in the commissions of the previous autumn to try the rebels and to seize their land. Richard Edgecombe's land in the south-west had been seized by Edward Redmane, who also took the cattle and sheep of a lesser, and otherwise unknown, Cornish rebel, John Bartelet.[3] Any legal deficiencies in the seizure of land after the rebellion were dealt with by a further act enabling the king to make grants of the land forfeited by those attainted, even if the requisite inquiries into its ownership had not been completed.

None of the victims of the protectorate features in the acts of parliament. Rivers, Grey and Vaughan had been tried at Pontefract before their execution and their land had been forfeited already. Hastings had received no trial, and nor was he now mentioned in the Act. On 23 July 1483, during his post-coronation progress, Richard had reached agreement with William's widow Katherine, promising that he would be her good and gracious sovereign lord; that her husband would not be attainted; and that his land, together with two important wardships granted to him by Edward IV, would not be seized but preserved in her keeping for their son Edward.[4] Katherine was a Neville, the sister of Richard, Earl of Warwick, the 'Kingmaker', although this is unlikely to have been the whole reason for her favoured treatment. It may have been tacit recognition on Richard's part that Hastings' death had been, in more senses than one, a bad move.

The king also took the occasion of parliament to woo his subjects. No lay taxation was requested, and that granted in January 1483 by Edward IV's last parliament and due to be levied at midsummer that year was left uncollected. The only cash levy collected in these early months of the reign had been the subsidy on aliens (foreign residents) also granted in the January 1483 parliament. Richard also announced his repudiation of benevolences, the unpopular 'free' cash gifts extorted by his late brother from the well-to-do. All this generosity was in spite of Richard's decidedly wobbly financial position. Although contemporary commentators are adamant that Edward had left a great treasure, in cash terms at least this was not the case, and the anxieties articulated in the January 1483 parliament about the cost of the royal household confirm that things had not been as rosy then as the Continuator, for one, assumed.[5]

The repudiation of another of Edward IV's financial expedients is also telling. Edward, or his officials, had in recent years been using the duchy of Lancaster as a test bed for improvements in royal revenue-raising. The January 1483 parliament had seen the formal introduction of a new policy towards wardships (the custody of orphaned children and their lands) in the duchy. Crown tenants there who held their lands by knight service (an obligation to fight for the king when summoned) were to be forbidden from putting the custody of the heir, and hence of his land, into the hands of trustees. Instead, wardship in those circumstances was to pass directly to the crown. Richard now revoked the policy: 'notwithstanding that he conceiveth the said act to be to his great profit . . . having more affection to the common weal of this his realm and of his subjects than to his own singular profit'.[6] Although there are indications later in the reign that Richard, like his brother, became interested in cranking up the exploitation of such 'feudal' rights (later to be ruthlessly exploited by Henry VII) he was also well aware that the duchy connection in the north was a significant element in his personal power base. His ally Sir Ralph Ashton – put out of office as receiver of Pickering by the duchy council in May 1480 for failing to answer for the revenues – had apparently been able just to stay put. Richard's almost immediate replacement of Edward's highly efficient chancellor of the duchy, Thomas Thwaites (who was sent off to be treasurer of Calais), by his own retainer Thomas Metcalfe (whose administrative grip on the duchy seems to have proved feeble) strongly suggests that the duchy was now to be run primarily as a royal support network rather than as a revenue stream.[7]

Other beneficiaries of the parliament included English merchants, who were offered some vehemently protectionist measures which Edward IV, anxious for good relations with Burgundy in particular, had always tried to duck. Royal allies were of course rewarded: Francis, Viscount Lovell, Richard's chamberlain, and Sir James Tyrell, his master of horse, benefited from the fall of Richard Grey and the south-western rebel Thomas Arundel respectively. The Earl of Northumberland was another, petitioning as 'a true liegeman of the king, who had always been of humble, true and due obedience and always would be', for the reversal of the attainder of his ancestors in the reign of Henry IV.[8] The collegiate chapel of Acaster and its attached school, founded by Robert Stillington, Bishop of Bath and Wells, had a grant of forty acres of land confirmed. Stillington has been seen by some commentators as the *éminence grise* of Richard's seizure of power: the source of the precontract story and the author of the *titulus regius*, although if so the confirmation seems a rather modest reward for services rendered.[9]

In these early months of 1484 opposition to the new regime was apparently quiescent. The rebels' land and office had been redistributed wholesale to create a power base for Richard's own associates – predominantly although not exclusively northern incomers – in the regions most affected.

While parliament was still in session, a draft letter of pardon was drawn up in the signet office for future use and there was a steady trickle of those suspected of involvement covering themselves by seeking and receiving a general pardon.[10] From May attainted rebels began to enter bonds for good behaviour as a preliminary to receiving pardon. The going rate was 1,000 marks, guaranteed by family members and associates, and the standard condition was that the former rebel should be of true and good bearing towards the king, and serve him in war and peace. Some were given additional conditions: to live with a kinsman loyal to the king, in the case of Thomas Lewkenor; or not to enter Kent without licence, in the case of Nicholas Gaynesford.[11]

It is not only with hindsight that this apparent hiatus in opposition can be recognized as illusory. Henry Tudor's credibility had been significantly enhanced, and he had become a crucial pawn in the complex diplomacy between England, France and Brittany. He had already received some backing for his 1483 invasion from Duke Francis of Brittany, and the level of the duke's financial support to the English exiles was now increased. Richard responded by stepping up action against Breton shipping in the Channel to put pressure on Duke Francis.

He also took steps to bring Edward IV's daughters, who were still in sanctuary with their mother, into his own keeping. On 1 March 1484, the king reached an agreement to that effect with Elizabeth Woodville. Richard's side of the bargain is set out in a long list of promises to the girls, beginning with security of life, no 'ravishment or defilement' or imprisonment in the Tower of London or elsewhere. The key clause from the king's point of view is that he would find husbands for 'them as now be marriageable'. The husbands provided would be 'gentlemen born', who would be charged 'lovingly to love and treat them as their wives and my kins-women'.[12] The promise was made in the presence of the Lords Spiritual and Temporal, and the mayor and aldermen of London; an indication both of Elizabeth Woodville's sus-picions and of how much was riding for the king on control of her daughters' marriages. The Continuator places the girls' emergence from sanctuary earlier, during the parlia-ment session, and before another occasion when Richard also summoned 'almost all the Lords Spiritual and Tem-poral and the leading knights and gentlemen of the king's household', this time to take an oath to accept his only son Edward as his heir if he were to die.[13] The episode gave the author occasion to philosophize sourly on the vanity of human plans when, early in April, the prince died aged ten at Middleham after a short illness.

The king and queen, at Nottingham when they heard the news, were frantic with grief. But alongside their personal response the death demanded political action. With his son's passing Richard's own dynastic position had become perilously insecure. The oath had shown the importance he attached to having a recognized successor; now he was without one. The Warwick-based historian John Rous thought that Clarence's son Edward, the Earl of Warwick, was subsequently acknowledged as heir, but he is a lone voice in this.[14] Warwick had been barred in the *titulus regius* and if now recognized as heir should arguably have been king in the first place. In a very thin field the most plausible candidate was the eldest of Richard's nephews: John, Earl of Lincoln, the son of the king's sister Elizabeth, Duchess of Suffolk. After Richard's accession his ducal council had in effect remained in being, staffed by some of the same officials and now apparently based in Prince Edward's northern household at Sheriff Hutton (Yorkshire). Lincoln seems to have stepped into the dead prince's shoes in that respect, becoming the head of the council in the north and taking over its officials. This can be read as an endorsement of his status as *de facto* the king's likely successor.[15] Given the importance Richard attached to keeping his hold on that region, it is also significant that Lincoln had virtually no northern interests of his own, beyond the ancestral connection of the de la Poles with Hull.

The breathing space brought by the collapse of Buckingham's rebellion had been brief. By July 1484, Richard was aware of renewed opposition in the south-west, and sent a powerful commission, headed by John, Lord Scrope of Bolton, who had become his right-hand man in the region, to investigate. In London in the same month the West Country rebel William Collingbourne was pinning up ballads of seditious language – although the only one to survive is on the face of it relatively harmless: 'The Cat, the Rat and Lovell our Dog rule all England under the Hog'. It pointed the finger at three of the king's leading (and very richly rewarded) allies: William Catesby, Richard Ratcliffe and Francis Lovell (whose heraldic badge was a dog). The Hog was, of course, Richard himself, whose own heraldic badge was a boar. More seriously, Collingbourne and his ally John Turberville, a kinsman of John Morton, had sent a messenger to Henry Tudor urging him to invade through Poole in Dorset and were planning a rising in the West Country to coincide with his arrival. Nothing came of that, or of the other outbreaks of unrest which came to the king's attention over the summer, and lent urgency to his efforts to winkle Tudor out of Brittany.

By September those efforts seemed close to success, helped by the temporary incapacity of Tudor's protector Duke Francis which had put power into the hands of the duke's treasurer, Pierre Landais. In that month William Catesby (Richard's Chancellor of the Exchequer and the 'Cat' of Collingbourne's rhyme) arrived in Brittany with the intention of taking Tudor back to England, but the rebel John Morton, then in Flanders, got wind of the plan in time to warn Tudor, who fled across the border into France. Richard's plan had thus backfired on him very badly. English relations with France still remained strained and the new king, Charles VIII, was delighted to gain possession of so potent a weapon. By October, Tudor had made his way to the French court; in the following month, Charles agreed to underwrite the cost of an invasion of England.

Tudor's arrival at the French court coincided with news of disaffection within the English enclave of Calais. At the end of October, Richard had been alerted to a plan to rescue the Lancastrian Earl of Oxford, John de Vere, imprisoned in the 1470s for rebellion against Edward IV, from Hammes, one of the Calais forts. The king immediately ordered the earl to be shipped back to England, but the command arrived too late. At the beginning of November the lieutenant of Hammes, James Blount, had freed de Vere and gone with

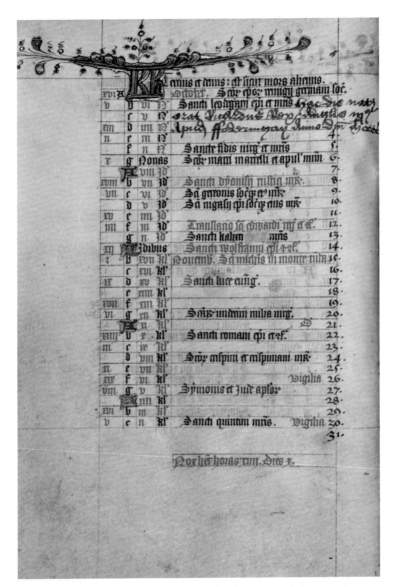

1. Richard's birthdate entered in the calendar for October in his own book of hours.

2. Middleham castle in Wensleydale, the centre of Richard's northern power base as duke of Gloucester.

3. The royal court: a wall painting in Eton College chapel, produced during the Yorkist period.

4. The Yorkist royal family. Richard is the figure in blue and miniver to the left of the king Edward IV.

5. Richard III as king: the earliest of the surviving portraits, but still painted a generation after his death.

6. Richard III seated in majesty in parliament, with members of the upper house around him.

7. Richard and his wife Anne. Her robe shows her heraldry as heiress of the earl of Warwick as well as the royal arms.

8. Richard's letter to the chancellor, bishop John Russell, concerning Buckingham's defection. The scrawled words in the margin are in the king's own handwriting.

9. Richard's badge was the boar, here represented in painted glass in St Martin with Gregory church in Micklegate, York.

10. The boar badge was also distributed among his followers in a mass-produced version.

11. Another, more elite version of the boar, pendant from the Yorkist livery collar of Ralph Fitzherbert of Norbury (Derbs), who died in 1484.

12. Richard as Shakespeare's 'bunched-back toad'. A statue that used to stand in the so-called 'King Richard III's House' on Sandgate, Scarborough.

him to join Tudor in France, accompanied by the porter of Calais, John Fortescue. Both men had been esquires of Richard's body and both were to be knighted by Tudor at his landing in 1485.[16] Disloyalty within Calais, a potential springboard for invasion of England, was deeply worrying and Richard immediately began an overhaul of the officials there, all of whom had been inherited from the Hastings regime. The Governor of Calais, John, Lord Dynham, survived the purge but Richard inserted a level of command above him, making his illegitimate son John captain of Calais and its three fortresses. The latter went to Calais, but was to have only limited authority there until he turned twenty-one and effective power probably rested with some form of council, analogous to the northern council formerly 'headed' by Prince Edward.[17]

The defections in Calais were telling evidence of Tudor's enhanced credibility. So too was the concurrent unrest in the east of England. Nothing came of this – Tudor was not yet ready to make a move – but it was potentially more threatening than the flurries of opposition earlier in the summer. It began with an armed rising in Colchester led by Sir William Brandon and his two sons, one of whom, William junior, had been attainted the previous year, but received a pardon in March. Other rebels who had thought it worth securing a pardon in spring also subsequently reneged. Among them was William Berkeley of Beverston (Gloucestershire), pardoned on the surety of John, Lord Stourton, and his uncle Edward Berkeley in March 1484 to be of good bearing and live where the king chose. By the following March, the money had been deemed forfeit. The previously loyal were also beginning to reconsider their position. One of the Brandons' allies was John Risley, an esquire of the king's body, who had earlier been rewarded with land forfeited by one of the 1483 rebels. Other royal household men inherited from Edward IV followed, including his keeper of the wardrobe, Piers Curteis.[18] Richard's following on all fronts seemed to be dribbling away. By the end of the year it was being confidently reported by the king's spies that Henry Tudor would invade in the following summer.

Amid the gathering danger, Richard celebrated his second Christmas lavishly, going crowned at Epiphany 'as though at his original coronation'.[19] It was at the feast on this occasion that Richard offered to give Southwark to the city of London and contribute £10,000 to build a wall around it. The offer was recorded by the city in its *Journal*, but nothing ever came of it and it is hard to resist the conclusion that the king was drunk when he made it.[20] The gift was certainly beyond his power to make, given the existing jurisdictions there, but its size has some affinity with grants that he *did* make: the rewards heaped on Buckingham, for instance, or his open-handed distribution of forfeited rebel land. One list of his grants, itself incomplete, itemizes land collectively valued at over £12,000; this in a society where the possession of land worth £40 would sustain the status of a knight.[21] Richard was equally generous with cash. Many of the crown estates were loaded with extra annuities, more, in some cases, than could comfortably be met from the available revenue. Open-handedness, largesse, was a chivalric virtue, but in Richard's case it was tipping over into the vice of prodigality.

The Continuator's verdict on the festive revelry was predictably negative. Too much time was given to singing and dancing, and to 'vain exchanges of clothing' between the queen and Edward's daughter Elizabeth.[22] This last was apparently interpreted by observers as evidence that Richard was thinking of wedding his niece once released from his marriage by the queen's death. Anne may by now have been a seriously sick woman, although there is no firm identification of her illness. She died on 16 March 1485 and immediately rumours began circulating that Richard did indeed intend to marry his niece. The version that reached France was that Richard *had* married her; news which Polydore Vergil claimed 'pinched Henry by the very stomach',[23] as well it might, given how much of his Yorkist support was riding on the match. It is possible that Richard did seriously consider such a match. He urgently needed to remarry in order to secure an heir of his body, and marrying Elizabeth would also neutralize her own claim to the throne. In fulfilment of his promise to find husbands for Edward IV's daughters he had already earmarked one for the second daughter – Cecily – but finding a 'safe' husband for Elizabeth was very much more problematic.[24]

It is clear that some of Richard's closest advisers thought that the story had substance. Richard Ratcliffe (the Rat of Collingbourne's rhyme) and William Catesby apparently argued vehemently against the idea to the king's face and insisted that he deny the intention publicly. They claimed that it would alienate the northerners, given that Queen Anne was the Earl of Warwick's daughter, and that such a marriage would in any case be incestuous. According to the

Continuator they were able to wheel out a dozen doctors of divinity to argue that even the pope could not dispense from the ban on uncle/niece matrimony. Richard, whatever his own intentions may have been, caved in. On 30 March 1485, in the great hall of the Hospital of St John, in the presence of the mayor and aldermen of London and a crowd of lords and others, the king stated his grief and displeasure at the claim that he had had his wife poisoned (an escalation of the accusation) so that he could marry Elizabeth. It had never entered his mind to do either thing and he charged all those present to cease telling such untruths. Anyone repeating the story was to be imprisoned until they revealed from whom they had heard it.[25]

According to the Continuator, the opposition of Ratcliff and Catesby was rooted in their fear that, were Elizabeth to become queen, she might at some point take her revenge on those behind the death of Rivers and Richard Grey. Behind this anxiety lies a development that the Continuator fails to make explicit: the progressive rehabilitation of surviving members of the Woodville family and their circle. The attention paid to Elizabeth over Christmas may well have been the first indication that Richard was feeling his way towards this rapprochement. On 12 January, Richard Woodville, Elizabeth's uncle, and the Woodville associate Sir John Fogge bound themselves in the sum of 1,000 marks to bear themselves well and faithfully towards the king. Fogge's pardon followed the next month, with a grant of some of his forfeited land. Woodville's pardon was granted in March, along with that of his fellow rebel and Woodville associate Richard Haute of Ightham.[26] Not all the pardons issued under the great seal in these months can necessarily be taken at face value. Some look more like bargaining counters: an invitation to the rebel concerned to open negotiations. But those associated with bonds for good behaviour can be taken seriously. Before Robert Clifford, one of those involved in the unrest of October 1484, received his general pardon, three Londoners had bound themselves that he would bear himself well towards the king and if anything affecting the king should come to his notice, would declare it to the king or his council.

The efficacy of the policy, at least as far as the erstwhile queen, Elizabeth Woodville, was concerned, is evidenced by her persuading her son Dorset to abandon Henry Tudor and return to England, although his escape was to be foiled by another of the 1483 rebels, Humfrey Cheyne. Her reputation, in the eyes of Henry VII and his chroniclers, was never to recover. Later in the year Tudor neutralized the now-suspect Dorset by leaving him as pledge for the money lent him by Charles VIII. The other pledge was John Bourchier, the former ward of the rebel Giles Daubeney (which explains his presence in France), but also the stepson of Richard's loyal esquire of the body John Sapcotes. Familial ties were complex, and so, necessarily, were loyalties. Richard Woodville had made his peace with the king; his surviving brothers, Lionel and Edward, stuck with Tudor. Families were hedging their bets – unsurprisingly in the context. This went both ways. Rebels made their peace with the crown – although the example of men like William Berkeley had shown how provisional this might be – and Yorkist loyalty continued to seep away from Richard III. Whether alienated by the manner of Richard's seizure of power, or by the growing dominance of his former retainers at both a national and local level, men were increasingly reconsidering their allegiance.

By the early months of 1485 the king was in a vicious circle. His long-term security demanded both that he hold the loyalty of those of his brother's men who had initially supported him and that he win back the disaffected from their support for Henry Tudor. But the shock of the 1483 rising, which had pushed him into an increasing dependence on his ducal connection, left him unwilling in the short term to lose the security this offered, even though the newcomers were demonstrably alienating local opinion. He recognized the need to conciliate opponents and some of the former rebels who made their peace with him in these months were, like Sir John Fogge, given a small part of their land back. But it is clear that Richard was not prepared to trust them with authority: none of them returned to the local commissions of the peace or received grants of royal office.

By this period, too, the king's financial difficulties were mounting. From his brother he had inherited a war against Scotland and a naval war against France, both of which he had continued. In the first half of 1484 there were English fleets in both the Channel and the North Sea. The Scottish conflict was a cause in which he had been closely involved, and he only grudgingly wound it down into a truce, dragging his feet over negotiations.[27] The conflict with France remained ongoing and entered a new phase with Charles's endorsement of Tudor's claim to the throne. While Tudor was still in Brittany, 1,000 English archers had been raised for the duchy's defence – the unstated *quid pro quo* being the handing over of Tudor, although he had made his escape in time and the money was in effect wasted. Suppressing Buckingham's rebellion had also involved significant military expenditure. Richard's open-handedness and liking for lavish display cannot have helped the situation.

Against these mounting costs, the king's forgoing of parliamentary taxation began to look increasingly quixotic. Early in 1485 he was forced to approach his subjects for a loan: a clear indication of the seriousness of his financial position. After his ringing rejection of benevolences in parliament as 'new and unlawful inventions and inordinate covetise', this inevitably jarred.[28] Richard was not breaking the letter of his undertaking. The essence of the benevolence was that it was an outright gift. Loans were, rather, intended to be repaid and a first instalment of that repayment was promised at Martinmas (11 November). But it was still an uncomfortable move and there may well have been doubts about the likelihood of repayment – in which case a loan would turn into a benevolence in all but name. The first letters, some to named individuals and others blank, went out in February, aiming to raise around £10,000. In the following month further letters had the target of £15,000. How much was actually raised is unclear. What *is* clear is that individuals approached by the king's collectors coughed up less than they had been asked for. Two-thirds seems to have been the going rate – thus a request for £100 netted 100 marks (£66 13s 4d). This was probably expected. More striking is the small number of men recorded in the Exchequer as having paid anything at all.[29] Unless other loans were going into the king's chamber, the records of which are lost, the appeal to 'every true Englishman' to contribute to the defence of the realm seems to have been falling on deaf ears. On lay ears, that is; the Church was more responsive and in February a convocation of the province of Canterbury granted the king the tax of a tenth 'for the defence of the realm and church of England'.[30] It was to be payable in two instalments, at midsummer 1485 and 1486.

At the same time Richard stepped up his efforts to extract money from the crown estate. A surviving memorandum from October 1484 was headed 'A remembrance made as well for hasty levy of the king's revenues growing of all his possessions and hereditaments as for the profitable estate and governance of the same possessions'.[31] Now, in spring 1485, he became more proactive. Commissioners began to be sent out to inquire into all the potential sources of cash which could be tapped by exploiting the king's rights of lordship. As was to become apparent under Henry VII, who brought this practice to a fine art, the potential gains were huge. This was true not only in cash terms – Richard extracted £1,000 from Sir William Say for failing to prevent the marriage of a ward before the requisite permission had been received – it could also serve as a useful way of putting pressure on individuals. Trialled in the duchy of Lancaster under Edward IV, this was now to be rolled out more widely, starting with the disaffected south-west – which suggests that the punitive possibilities of the practice may also have been in Richard's mind.[32]

Against this financial background, the wisdom of backing

away from outright war seems obvious. But Richard did
not want to back away. What he needed was to assert his
God-given right to kingship by a major victory in battle.
The dissolution of Buckingham's rebellion had denied him
that. The Scottish conflict had not provided a set-piece
battle and was unlikely to do so now as it wound down.
France was potentially more promising. In August 1484,
when a French attack on Calais was anticipated, Richard,
in a letter to the Earl of Arundel urging him to see to the
defence of the Cinque Ports, self-identified as 'that prince,
which for the defence of this realm and all the possessions
of the crown of England is disposed to employ his own
royal person as far as any king hath done in years past'.[33]
There is an echo here of Edward IV's address given 'with
his own mouth' to the Commons in his first parliament
and its reference to 'my own body ... the which shall
always be ready for your defence, never sparing nor letting
[holding back] for no jeopardy'.[34] But the 1484 attack
never materialized, and would hardly have constituted a
major confrontation if it had. By 1485 only an invasion by
Henry Tudor offered Richard the possibility of a decisive
endorsement of his kingship.

No one was in any doubt that the invasion would come.
Where it would come, in spite of the efforts of Richard's
spies, was more doubtful. Francis, Viscount Lovell, the
king's friend and chamberlain – the role Hastings had
filled in Edward IV's reign – was sent to guard the south
coast around Southampton. According to the Continuator,
this was because of the misinterpretation of a prophecy
that Henry would land at 'Milford' (as, in the event he did,

but at Milford Haven) and there was thought to be a place of that name near Southampton. The choice of the Southampton area as Lovell's base was, however, more securely grounded than this allows. Richard had regarded the port as a likely trouble spot when tracking down the Woodvilles and their allies during his protectorate and its role as one of the *foci* of Buckingham's rebellion had led to the temporary suspension of the city's liberties and the attainder of its mayor at the time, Walter Williams.[35]

Richard left Westminster for the last time on 11 May 1485, celebrating the feast of the Ascension at Windsor the next day. From there he travelled to his mother's residence at Berkhamsted, where he may have stayed a few days, and then via Kenilworth to Nottingham: the castle where he had spent so much of the reign. He arrived there in the second week of June. All the military preparations had long been made. A proclamation against the leading rebels – Piers Courtenay, Dorset, Jasper Tudor, Oxford, Edward Woodville and their captain, 'one Harry, late calling himself Earl of Richmond' – had been composed on 7 December, to be sent to every county. The king's subjects, 'like good and true Englishmen', were urged to the defence of themselves, their wives, children, goods and inheritances. Commissions of array had been issued the next day.[36] Now all Richard had to do was wait.

5
Defeat

Although the 1483 rebellion and subsequent outbreaks of opposition had failed, they had done so by dissolution rather than defeat. Many of the leading rebels had escaped; initially to Brittany; later, with Henry Tudor, to France. Others had simply disappeared into the landscape or remained unidentified. Some who had initially made their peace with the regime after Buckingham's rebellion were back in opposition by the end of 1484. More damaging, former household servants of Edward IV who had apparently transferred smoothly into Richard's service in 1483 were increasingly reconsidering their position, or were suspected of doing so. At least five esquires of Richard's body – as their office suggests, among the most intimate of his servants – and the keeper of his great wardrobe, all inherited from the service of Edward IV, were to suffer forfeiture for treason committed *after* 1483. It was to be the Bosworth campaign that brought into the open the full extent of that seepage of loyalty. But Richard, having burnt his fingers once by keeping his brother's servants in office at the beginning of his reign rather than turning to his own retainers, as he did thereafter, must surely have been increasingly conscious of the risk.

He was certainly suspicious of the Stanleys, who had managed to duck any overt involvement in the 1483 rebellion. Richard had then rewarded Lord Thomas generously for his inactivity (for it was no more than that), appointing his 'right welbeloved cousin and councillor' as constable of England in Buckingham's place, and making him a knight of the garter. Stanley was later to add the stewardship of the royal household to his roles.[1] Royal largesse in the form of forfeited land and office was also extended to Thomas's younger brother William, a knight of the king's body. But the inherent ambiguity of the Stanley position was underlined by Thomas's possession for life of the estates forfeited by his attainted wife Margaret Beaufort and the king remained wary. Thomas was not raised to the peerage, and the brothers were never allowed to extend their grip on the duchy of Lancaster, which had formed so vital a part of Richard's own power in the north. The king's favour in that region remained directed rather to the Harrington family, the Stanleys' long-standing rivals.[2] As Henry Tudor's plans took firmer shape, and Thomas Stanley sought permission to leave court to visit his estates, Richard insisted on keeping his son and heir, George, Lord Strange, hostage as surety for his father's good behaviour. The king was taking precautions against an invasion which was now recognized as inevitable.

On 7 August, Tudor's ships, having safely bypassed Lovell's fleet off Southampton, landed at Milford Haven. South Wales, apart from Pembroke, under the command of the royal esquire Richard Williams, was effectively an open door. The king may have been lulled into a false sense of security by the region's failure to come out in support of Buckingham, and in the aftermath of that rebellion he seems to have given relatively little attention to overhauling the structure of office-holding there, which remained very largely that established by Edward IV. A significant exception had been his deployment of Sir James Tyrell in the region; but Tyrell had been despatched to Calais to sort out the disaffection there the previous year, and his officials in Glamorgan and Morgannwg were simply ordered to go on obeying him, 'notwithstanding that the king sendeth him to Guines'.[3] It is unclear whether this was misplaced optimism or dawning recognition that Richard's power base there was too thin for comfort.

Although Tudor's force faced no opposition as they headed north through Wales, any potential supporters were initially slow to show their hand. The English element among the troops was at this stage numerically small, its high-profile leaders all former exiles and probably not in a position to levy their own men quickly. The bulk of the force was made up of mercenaries provided by the French king Charles VIII. There was probably a Scottish element within that cohort and Tudor was also able to garner some Welsh support as he advanced. On 15 August, having crossed the border into England, they arrived at Shrewsbury, where the city's bailiff – Thomas Mitton, a royal esquire rewarded less than two years earlier for his good service against Buckingham with a hereditary grant of the duke's Shropshire castle of Caus – opened the gates to them with only a token show of opposition.[4] From there Tudor's army headed east, to Newport and Stafford, where William Stanley arrived for a consultation. Lord Stanley was by this time in the field with his troops but, characteristically keeping his options open, was apparently retreating before the rebel forces.

News of Henry Tudor's landing had reached Richard at the royal hunting lodge of Bestwood, near Nottingham, by 11 August and arrangements to levy troops swung into action. Commissions of array to all the English counties – appointing men to raise forces against those 'open murderers, adulterers and extortioners' who intended 'the most cruel murders, slaughters, robberies and disinheritings that ever were seen in any Christian realm' – had gone out on 8 December 1484.[5] On 22 June this state of alert was ramped up, and the knights, esquires and gentlemen named in the commissions were warned to be ready at an hour's notice to muster their forces. The individual letters of summons, which finally triggered the whole operation, went out under the king's signet and sign manual on 11 August. Recipients were ordered to attend on the king with their promised troops 'all manner [of] excuses set apart, upon pain of forfeiture to us of all that you may forfeit and lose' – a command interpreted by the Continuator as a threat that absentees from battle would lose their life as well as their lands and possessions.[6] Time was tight. The Duke of Norfolk, who cannot have received the order much before 13 August, summoned his men to muster at Bury St Edmunds on the evening of Tuesday the 16th. That was the day one of the duke's recruits, Thomas Longe of Ashwellthorpe (Norfolk), made his will, 'going forth unto the king's host at Nottingham to battle'.[7] It was also the day that the king finally set out from Nottingham, having postponed his departure in honour of the feast of the Assumption on the Monday.

Both armies moved relatively slowly, waiting for more men to come in. Tudor had reached Lichfield on 20 August, and Richard had moved his forces to Leicester by the evening of the same day. Significant numbers of his supporters were yet to arrive. On 16 August the city of York had written to the king asking what military support he needed, which suggests that active recruitment there had not yet got fully under way.[8] The commissions of array in the northern counties were headed by the Earl of Lincoln, in his capacity as head of the council in the north, with Henry Percy, Earl of Northumberland, as his second in command (apart from the East Riding where their positions were reversed). Lincoln had latterly been based with the king at Nottingham, and it has been suggested that Percy was less than enthusiastic (or less than efficient) about recruiting. The York contingent was not despatched until the 19th and other northern levies may have been equally slow off the mark. Robert Morton of Bawtry made his will on 20 August, 'going to maintain our most excellent king Richard III against the rebellion raised against him in this land'.[9]

The royal army that reached Leicester in battle array that day was judged by the Continuator to constitute the greatest number of fighting men ever seen in England on one side. The figures of foreign commentators are even more exaggerated (and implausible).[10] There is no question that Richard's army was significantly bigger than Henry's. But it is clear from all accounts, including the Continuator's own, that no-shows and desertions were rife, quite apart from the continuing ambiguity over the intention of the Stanleys and their supporters. At least one commissioner of array, John Biconnell in Somerset, simply took his men to join the rebel forces and was knighted by Henry.[11] The constable of the Tower, Sir Robert Brackenbury, a loyal workhorse of the regime, brought with him 'many gentlemen of the order of knighthood whom [the king] had in suspicion', among them Walter Hungerford, a 1483 rebel who had been pardoned in April 1484. He, along with Brackenbury's other *de facto* prisoners, defected before arriving at the battle.[12] They reputedly urged Brackenbury to go with them, but he refused and was to die in the battle. So did John Howard, Duke of Norfolk – warned, according to later stories, by a note pinned to his tent on the morning of the battle, not to be too bold 'for Dickon thy master is bought and sold'.[13]

Richard and his companions must already have been acutely aware of support draining away. This explains the threatening rhetoric of the letters of 11 August – very different in tone from the proclamation of 6 December, in which Richard had called upon his subjects 'like good and true Englishmen to endeavour themselves with all their powers for defence of themselves, their wives, children, goods and inheritances'.[14] Their uneasiness perhaps helps to explain the disarray in which the royal camp found itself on the morning of 22 August. There was a muddle over the provision of the elements for the celebration of Mass – an incident confirmed by an eye-witness as well as being emphasized by the Continuator and all subsequent writers – so that Richard faced battle without having received the Sacrament.[15] Confidence among the troops can hardly have been raised by rumours that the king had had a nightmare about demons surrounding him – a story mentioned first by the Continuator, picked up by all subsequent writers and reaching its apogee in Shakespeare's *Richard III*, where the 'legion of foul fiends' are augmented by the manifestation of the king's victims.

Fears about the battle's outcome seem to have prompted evasive action. The Continuator claims that many of Richard's trusted northerners fled before coming to blows, and Polydore Vergil, another well-informed source, also speaks of desertions as the battle got under way.[16] One Ricardian commander who is known not to have engaged his forces was Northumberland. Various interpretations of this are possible, and the Continuator's phrasing is studiedly noncommittal about why no blows were struck. The authors of the most recent reconstruction of the battle have made out a plausible case that Northumberland was blocked from engaging by the movement of other forces in the field.[17] Or he could have been hedging his bets. Henry VII was evidently unsure about this too – the earl, although escaping attainder, was imprisoned and only released, and his offices restored, towards the end of the year.

Recent reassessment of the battle has focused on the fate of Richard himself. Chronicle accounts differ in detail but all, even the most hostile, agree that he died bravely in battle. The Continuator was clear: 'he received many mortal wounds, and like a spirited and most courageous prince, fell in battle on the field and not in flight.' This is true, but not quite the whole story. The account by the Burgundian chronicler Jean Molinet that he was hacked to death captures the reality more closely.[18] Analysis of the bones now identified as Richard's strongly suggests that he had not simply been cut down in the heat of battle. The picture instead is of 'capture, immobilisation and efficient dispatch and finally humiliation'. The last is a reference to the fact that the dead body was viciously mutilated after it had been stripped.[19] It was then, as all the chroniclers agree, thrown naked across a horse's back to be carried into Leicester, where it may have remained on display for a few days before being buried, uncoffined, in the chancel of the church of the Greyfriars.

It is possible to make excuses for what happened on that Monday in August. Pitched battles were notoriously chancy affairs, in which the 'wrong' (that is, the apparently weaker) side might win. Medieval military commanders generally preferred to wage wars of attrition, although this never played well in the context of civil war and the Wars of the Roses were largely fought out in set-piece battles. Richard may have made strategic errors in grouping his troops. Men on his side may, for whatever reason, have been unwilling to engage with the enemy. Or, as the king's defenders have argued, he was defeated because he had been betrayed. All these explanations are plausible (and not mutually exclusive), but they beg the question of why Richard was facing an army in the first place – an army that was in motivation quintessentially a Yorkist force.

That a young man with no claim to the throne – beyond being the grandson of Henry V's widow and the son of a great-great-granddaughter of Edward III – could in 1485 amass enough support to overthrow the reigning king can be seen as just the final stage in the cascade of depositions which followed that of Henry VI in 1461: a series of reversals that had made kingship itself seem contingent. But the opposition which brought down Richard III was not a reactivation of the Wars of the Roses, although the choice of figurehead might make it seem so. It was more truly a violent splintering of the House of York, which fatally divided the Yorkist polity far beyond any rifts that might have been caused previously by hostility to the family of Edward IV's queen. Simply put, the former servants of Edward IV rejected his brother's seizure of power. This was not immediately apparent, at least not to Richard himself, who enthusiastically took many of the household men of his brother into his service after his usurpation. Buckingham's rebellion was a devastating personal betrayal but it also convinced the king how little he could trust his brother's former servants (something to be confirmed by continuing desertions) and it was, famously, the promotion of his own northerners that was to become the crucial underpinning of his regime.

Richard had presented himself in spring 1483 as the preserver of the *good* government of his brother in the face of Woodville corruption, but this did not last very long. The assumed death of the princes must inevitably have sunk his claim on Yorkist loyalties. But, earlier than that, his condemnation of the moral depravity of Edward's kingship, and the bastardization of his children in the *titulus regius*, was implicitly casting him as purifier rather than upholder.

This motif was to recur. It is articulated at length in the proclamation against the rebels in October 1483. Dorset was the main target, accused of 'damnably and without shame devour[ing], deflower[ing] and defoul[ing]' many and sundry maids, widows and wives; but the accusation of the 'damnable maintenance of vices and sin' was extended to all the rebels. Richard was later, in a letter to the bishops, to articulate his 'principal intent and fervent desire' as the advance of virtue and cleanliness of life and the repression of vice, but there is real venom, if not hysteria, in the abuse heaped upon his opponents.[20]

Unsurprisingly, relatively few of Edward's former allies were prepared to turn out for Richard at Bosworth. But if one tries to gauge the nature of Richard's support from the relatively small number of those attainted in Henry VII's first parliament (twenty-nine – significantly fewer than after Buckingham's rebellion), it is striking how few of those allies were northern, perhaps only around a quarter.[21] This probably reflects the facts that a proportion of the northern levies did not arrive in time and that Northumberland's forces, presumably predominantly northern, did not engage. There may also be a more damaging reason. Under his brother, Richard had been a virtually unassailable lord of the north. In that capacity he could be a generous good lord to his supporters. That remained true – arguably more true – after his accession when many of his supporters flocked south to share the spoils. But many of them – not all – were of relatively small standing in the north itself, heading away to make their fortune and, apparently, not recruited in support of him (or at least not making it back in time) in August 1485. The big names had less to gain; not only that, but they may have felt that the balance of power had tilted against them.

Richard did not mean to let go of the north. His ducal council there remained in being *de facto*, providing a structure for his continuing authority in the region, although little is known of its proceedings. Nominally headed initially by his son; after the prince's death the Earl of Lincoln was also essentially a royal figurehead. Northumberland and the new Earl of Westmorland, Ralph Neville (who inherited the earldom in 1484), were rewarded generously by Richard but their big gains were kept to forfeited land in the south and any extension of their authority in the north was slight.[22] Their enthusiasm for his regime, while stopping short of overt opposition, may have cooled.

That said, putting too much weight on the Act of Attainder may be misleading. Such acts were negotiable until the dissolution of parliament. As had been demonstrated in Richard's own parliament, it was possible for men to buy themselves out of inclusion. And the time between Bosworth on 22 August and the first meeting of Henry VII's parliament on 7 November had been long enough for pardons to be negotiated, as Northumberland had done. Given Henry's apparent willingness to be conciliatory (although this was clearly more limited in the case of his aristocratic opponents than lesser figures), the Act of Attainder can perhaps best be seen as a tally of the dead and the still disaffected rather than a full listing of Richard's supporters on the day.

Opposition from erstwhile Ricardians continued to surface over the next few years, initially focused on the claims of the Yorkist heir male: Clarence's son the young Earl of Warwick, who was in Henry's keeping. There was a rising by Richard's friend Francis, Viscount Lovell, and his associates in 1486, which came to nothing. More serious opposition gathered in 1487, headed by the Earl of Lincoln (whom Henry VII had pardoned in 1485) and drawing help from Ireland, where the plot was hatched, and Richard's sister Margaret of Burgundy. At its centre was the impersonation of the Earl of Warwick by the pretender Lambert Simnel. As the rebels advanced through Lancashire and, more particularly, Yorkshire they evidently drew in numbers of former Ricardians. Indeed this campaign can plausibly be seen, alien support notwithstanding, as a *Ricardian* counter-attack on the house of Tudor. It was to end in defeat at Stoke by a royal army that was essentially Yorkist in composition.

Francis Bacon's insistence that the memory of Richard III lay like lees in the bottom of men's hearts may well be true. But in the end most of Richard's servants preferred to make their peace with the new regime. How that transition was subsequently regarded by the individuals concerned is much harder to detect. Marmaduke Constable, a knight of Richard's body and given by him extensive authority in the duchy of Lancaster lands in the north Midlands, apparently wrote his service to Richard out of the record. His lengthy memorial in Flamborough Church (East Riding) lists his noteworthy deeds under Edward IV and Henry VII and says nothing at all about King Richard. Avery Cornburgh, who had risen through Edward IV's service from yeoman of the crown to esquire of the body and under-treasurer, offices he also held under Richard, was similarly silent about that part of his career, recording his service to kings Edward and Henry only.[23] At the other extreme is Sir Ralph Bygott, initially in the service of Queen Anne and at her death entering that of the king. He fought for Richard at Bosworth, and is the source of the reminiscence cited above about the confusion leading to the non-celebration of Mass that morning. He was wounded in the battle but survived and entered the service of Henry's mother, Margaret Beaufort. There he refused to listen to any criticism of his former master, an attitude which Margaret considered praiseworthy, 'to be ever more so true a servant to him'.[24]

Epilogue

The spectrum of opinion about Richard III must be the widest of any English king. He was bitterly hated in his own time but also capable of commanding great loyalty (*affection* is always more elusive in the historical record). The same division, toned down a bit at each extreme, still persists today between his critics and defenders. The former present him as a fiercely ambitious man, intent on preserving (and extending) the power he had enjoyed under his brother by brutally seizing the throne for himself. The latter are more inclined to see him as a man passionately committed to the house of York, fighting in defence of his brother's legacy against the self-aggrandizement of the Woodvilles. In the end the outcome of both interpretations is the same. His bitter, one could even say obsessive, attack on the decadence of the court during the Woodville regime was to destroy not only the Woodvilles, but the reputation of his dead brother the king and finally the house of York itself. However one chooses to interpret his actions, he can with justice be seen as a *failed* king, who in the end destroyed whatever it was that he had sought to rescue and preserve, losing his crown, and his life, in the process.

Notes

ABBREVIATIONS

Attreed	L. C. Attreed (ed.), *York House Books, 1461–1490*, 2 vols (Gloucester: Alan Sutton for Richard III and Yorkist History Trust, 1991)
Crowland	*The Crowland Chronicle Continuations 1459–1486*, ed. N. Pronay and J. Cox (London: Richard III and Yorkist History Trust, 1986)
EHR	*English Historical Review*
'Financial Memoranda'	R. Horrox (ed.), 'Financial Memoranda of the Reign of Edward V', *Camden Miscellany*, XXIX, Camden Fourth Series, 34 (London: Royal Historical Society, 1987)
Great Chronicle	A. H. Thomas and I. D. Thorley (eds), *The Great Chronicle of London* (Gloucester: Alan Sutton, 1983)
Harl. 433	*British Library Harleian Manuscript 433*, ed. R. Horrox and P. W. Hammond, 4 vols (Gloucester: Alan Sutton for the Richard III Society, 1979–83)
Horrox	R. Horrox, *Richard III: A Study of Service* (Cambridge: Cambridge University Press, 1989)
Mancini	Dominic Mancini, *The Usurpation of Richard III*, ed. C. A. J. Armstrong, 2nd edn (Oxford: Clarendon Press, 1969)
More	Thomas More, *The History of King Richard III*, ed. R. S. Sylvester (New Haven, CT: Yale University Press, 1963)
Patent Rolls	*Calendar of the Patent Rolls Preserved in the Public Record Office: Edward IV, Edward V, Richard III, 1476–1485* (London: HMSO, 1901)
PROME	*The Parliament Rolls of Medieval England, 1275–1504*, ed. C. Given-Wilson et al., 16 vols (Woodbridge: Boydell Press, 2005)
TNA	The National Archives, Kew
Vergil	*The Three Books of Polydore Vergil's English History*, ed. Henry Ellis (London: Camden Society, 1844)

PROLOGUE

1. Francis Bacon, *The History of the Reign of King Henry the Seventh*, ed. Roger Lockyer (London: Folio Society, 1971) p. 94.

I. THE YOUNGEST BROTHER

1. *PROME*, XIII, p. 11.
2. M. L. Kekewich et al. (eds), *The Politics of Fifteenth Century England: John Vale's Book* (Stroud: Sutton Publishing for Richard III and Yorkist History Trust, 1995), pp. 212–15.
3. Horrox, pp. 31–2; S. Cunningham, *Richard III: A Royal Enigma* (Kew, Richmond: National Archives, 2003), pp. 12–13.
4. Cunningham, *Richard III*, pp. 69–70; R. Somerville, *History of the Duchy of Lancaster*, vol. 1: *1265–1603* (Lancaster: Chancellor and Council of the Duchy of Lancaster, 1953), p. 257; *Calendar of Close Rolls Preserved in the Public Record Office: Edward IV*, vol. 2: *1468–1476* (London: HMSO, 1953), no. 535.
5. J. G. Nichols (ed.), *Chronicle of the Rebellion in Lincolnshire, 1470* (London: Camden Society, 1847).
6. J. Bruce (ed.), *Historie of the Arrivall of Edward IV into England* (London: Camden Society, 1838), p. 38.
7. P. D. Clark and P. N. R. Zutshi (eds), *Registers of the Apostolic Penitentiary*, vol. 2: *1464–1492*, Canterbury & York Society, 104 (Woodbridge: Boydell & Brewer, 2014), no. 1824.
8. C. D. Ross, *Edward IV* (London: Eyre Methuen, 1974), pp. 189–91.
9. *Sixth Report of the Royal Commission on Historical Manuscripts* (London: Eyre & Spottiswoode, 1877), pp. 223–4.
10. D. A. L. Morgan, 'The King's Affinity in the Polity of Yorkist England', *Transactions of the Royal Historical Society*, 5th Series, 23 (1973), p. 17.
11. TNA, DL 5/1 fo. 7.
12. M. Hicks, 'The Last Days of Elizabeth Countess of Oxford', *EHR*, 103 (1988), pp. 76–95; J. Ross, 'Richard, Duke of Gloucester and the de Vere Estates, 1462–85', *The Ricardian*, 15 (2005), pp. 20–32.
13. *Crowland*, pp. 145, 147.
14. Kekewich, *John Vale's Book*, pp. 212–15.
15. Mancini, pp. 64–5.
16. Ibid., pp. 62–3.
17. P. M. Kendall, *Richard the Third* (London: Allen & Unwin, 1955), pp. 125–7, was an early exponent of the argument.
18. *PROME*, XIV, pp. 425–8.
19. W. C. Metcalfe, *A Book of Knights* (London: Mitchell and Hughes, 1885), pp. 5–7.

2. THE PROTECTOR

1. *Great Chronicle*, p. 230.
2. *Crowland*, p. 159.
3. 'Financial Memoranda', p. 218.
4. *Harl. 433*, III, p. 2; A. F. Sutton, L. Visser-Fuchs and R. A. Griffiths (eds), *The Royal Funerals of the House of York at Windsor* (London: Richard III Society, 2005), pp. 14, 25, 38.

5. 'Financial Memoranda', p. 216.
6. Horrox, pp. 102–5.
7. A. Raine (ed.), *York Civic Records*, I, Yorkshire Archaeological Society Record Series, 98 (Leeds: 1938), pp. 73–5; Attreed, I, p. 284; P. W. Hammond and A. F. Sutton, *Richard III: The Road to Bosworth Field* (London: Constable, 1985), pp. 103–4; Kingston upon Hull Record Office, Bench Book, 3A, fo. 133v.
8. 'Financial Memoranda', pp. 216–17; *Kingsford's Stonor Letters and Papers 1290–1483*, ed. C. Carpenter (Cambridge: Cambridge University Press, 1996), no. 330.
9. *Great Chronicle*, p. 231; More, pp. 48–9.
10. More, pp. 47–8; *Great Chronicle*, p. 231.
11. *Harl. 433*, II, pp. 17–18.
12. *Crowland*, p. 159; Mancini, pp. 90–91.
13. *Crowland*, p. 159; Mancini, pp. 92–3.
14. *Crowland*, p. 159.
15. Carpenter (ed.), *Kingsford's Stonor Letters*, no. 331.
16. TNA, E 404/78/1/4; *Harl. 433*, I, pp. 8–15, 16–18, 28–33, 65.
17. *Harl. 433*, I, pp. 69–71. Richard also planned to give him a significant part of the duchy of Lancaster lands in the south: *Harl. 433*, II, pp. 2–4, and see Horrox, *Richard III*, p. 133.
18. *Great Chronicle*, p. 231–2; Mancini, pp. 94–5.
19. *PROME*, XV, pp. 13–18.
20. Ibid.
21. *Crowland*, p. 161.
22. *Harl. 433*, III, pp. 28–30.

3. BY THE GRACE OF GOD, KING

1. A. F. Sutton and P.W. Hammond (eds), *The Coronation of Richard III: The Extant Documents* (Gloucester and New York: Alan Sutton and St Martin's Press, 1983).
2. *The Complete Peerage*, 6 vols (Gloucester: Alan Sutton, 1982), II, pp. 133–5 (Berkeley, Earl of Nottingham); IV, pp. 610–12 (Howard, Duke of Norfolk); Ross, *Edward IV*, pp. 248–9.
3. R. Edwards, *The Itinerary of King Richard III 1483–1485* (London: Sutton Publishing for the Richard III Society, 1983), pp. 4–6.
4. Horrox, p. 148; J. B. Sheppard (ed.), *Christ Church Letters*, Camden Society, New Series, 19 (London: 1877), p. 46; A. Hanham, *Richard III and His Early Historians, 1483–1535* (London: Oxford University Press, 1975), p. 50; *Harl. 433*, III, p. 1.
5. J. Stow, *The Annales of England* (London: 1592), p. 762; T. Basin, *Histoire de Louis XI*, ed. C. Samaran and M. C. Garand, 3 vols (Paris: Belles-Lettres, 1963), III, pp. 234–5; *Crowland*, p. 163.
6. Mancini, pp. 92–3.
7. *Hall's Chronicle*, ed. Henry Ellis (London: J. Johnson, 1809), p. 490.
8. M. K. Jones and M. G. Underwood, *The King's Mother: Lady Margaret Beaufort* (Cambridge: Cambridge University Press, 1992), pp. 60–64.
9. *Harl. 433*, II, p. 7.
10. Attreed, II, p. 713.

11. *Harl. 433*, II, p. 13. He had also, four days previously, sold a wardship to his chief justice William Hussey for a down payment of 850 marks: ibid., pp. 13–14.

12. C. Ross, *Richard III* (London: Eyre Methuen, 1981), p. 142.

13. Attreed, I, p. 296, II, pp. 413–14; *Crowland*, p. 163; Vergil, pp. 198–9; TNA, C 81/1392/6.

14. TNA, E 404/78/2/4.

15. *PROME*, XV, pp. 24–9; Sutton and Hammond (eds), *Coronation*, pp. 270–74; L. Gill, *Richard III and Buckingham's Rebellion* (Stroud: Sutton Publishing, 1999), especially ch. 5; Horrox, ch. 3.

16. TNA, E 207/21/16/12.

17. As Richard travelled into the south-west, commissions of array continued to be issued until he reached Exeter on 13 November, when they were replaced by commissions of arrest.

18. *Crowland*, pp. 163–65; C. Rawcliffe, *The Staffords, Earls of Stafford and Dukes of Buckingham, 1394–1521* (Cambridge: Cambridge University Press, 1978), pp. 32–4.

19. J. Kirby (ed.), *The Plumpton Letters and Papers*, Camden Fifth Series, 8 (London: Royal Historical Society, 1996), no. 39.

20. *Harl. 433*, II, pp. 2–4.

21. *Crowland*, pp. 163–5; More, pp. 90–93.

22. TNA, KB 9/953/17.

23. TNA, C 81/1531/3.

24. TNA, E 404/78/3; E 404/78/40.

25. *Harl. 433*, II, p. 32.

26. *Calendar of Inquisitions Miscellaneous Preserved in the Public Record Office*, vol. 8: *1422–1485* (Woodbridge: Boydell Press, 2003), no. 480.

4. PICKING UP THE PIECES

1. *PROME*, XV, pp. 34–6.

2. Ibid., pp. 152–3.

3. TNA, KB 9/369/22; KB 9/1060/33.

4. *Harl. 433*, II, pp. 4–5. The grant worked its way only slowly through the system, not passing the great seal until 9 February 1485: *Patent Rolls*, p. 496.

5. The Continuator contradicts himself about the extent of Edward's treasure: *Crowland*, pp. 147–9, 161; *PROME*, XIV, pp. 404–5. At Edward's death there was £490 7s 8d in the Treasury and £710 in his chamber: 'Financial Memoranda', p. 219. This ignores the wealth tied up in plate.

6. *PROME*, XIV, pp. 432–3; XV, pp. 59–61.

7. TNA, DL 29/500/8100; DL 29/500/8103; C76/168 m. 10; DL 28/5/11 fo. 19v; DL 42/19 fos. 1v–2, 112; DL 42/20 fos. 3, 41, 59.

8. *PROME*, XV, pp. 39–48.

9. Ibid., pp. 48–9; the only contemporary reference to the bishop's role is supplied by the French chronicler Philippe de Commynes in his *Mémoires* (1524); Kendall gave the accusation a wider audience in his *Richard the Third*, pp. 215–18.

10. TNA, C81/1530/25; C81/1531/48.

11. TNA, C81/1531/48; *Calendar of Close Rolls Preserved in the Public Record Office: Edward IV, Edward V, Richard III, 1476–1485* (London: HMSO, 1954), nos. 1242, 1258–9; Horrox, pp. 273–5.

12. *Harl. 433*, III, p. 295.

13. *Crowland*, pp. 170–71.

14. John Rous, *Historia Regum Angliae*, ed. Thomas Hearne (Oxford: J. Fletcher and J. Pote, 1745), pp. 218–19.

15. *Harl. 433*, III, pp. 107–8, 114–16. Both documents (the ordinance for the council and that for the household) are undated, but the household (to be based at Sandal) was deemed to have been set up on the day Richard left Yorkshire: 24 July 1484.

16. TNA, C 81/1392/19; C 67/51 mm. 10, 18; *Harl. 433*, I, pp. 129–30, 138, 230.

17. TNA, C 76/169 m. 26; Thomas Rymer (ed.), *Foedera, Conventiones, Literae, et Cuiuscunque Generis Acta Publica*, vol. 12 (London: A. & J. Churchill, 1711), pp. 265–6; *Harl. 433*, I, p. 271.

18. Horrox, pp. 278–81, 283.

19. *Crowland*, p. 173.

20. A. F. Sutton, 'Richard III, the City of London and Southwark', in *Richard III: Crown and People*, ed. J. Petre (Gloucester: Alan Sutton, 1985), pp. 289–95.

21. *Harl. 433*, III, pp. 139–55.

22. *Crowland*, p. 175.

23. Vergil, p. 215. A graphic translation of the original Latin, *Henricum graviter mordere*.

24. Cecily was married to Ralph Scrope, the brother of Thomas, Lord Scrope of Upsall. The marriage was dissolved in 1486 to allow her marriage to John, Lord Welles: R. H. Helmholz, *Marriage Litigation in Medieval England* (New York: Cambridge University Press, 1975), p. 160 (n. 89); S. B. Chrimes, *Henry VII* (London: Eyre Methuen, 1972), pp. 35–6 (n. 2).

25. *Crowland*, p. 175.

26. TNA, C 244/136/92, 130, 132; C 237/51/14, 31; *Harl. 433*, I, pp. 267, 277, II, p. 50.

27. *Harl. 433*, III, pp. 47–8, 50–51, 71, 105–6.

28. *PROME*, XV, p. 58.

29. *Harl. 433*, III, pp. 128–30; TNA, E 401/951–2.

30. *Calendar of Fine Rolls Preserved in the Public Record Office*, vol. 21: *Edward IV, Edward V, Richard III, 1471–1485* (London: HMSO, 1961), nos. 880–82.

31. *Harl. 433*, III, pp. 118–20, printed in B. P. Wolffe, *The Crown Lands 1461–1536* (London: George Allen & Unwin, 1970), pp. 133–6.

32. TNA, E 401/951; *Patent Rolls*, pp. 543, 546.

33. TNA, C 81/1531/3.

34. *PROME*, XIII, pp. 63–4.

35. *Harl. 433*, II, p. 196; *Crowland*, pp. 176–7.

36. *Harl. 433*, III, pp. 124–5.

5. DEFEAT

1. *Patent Rolls*, pp. 367, 476; *Harl. 433*, I, p. 94. Stanley also received Buckingham's lordship of Kimbolton (Huntingdonshire) on the day of the duke's execution: ibid., II, p. 3.

2. Horrox, pp. 69–70; D. J. Clayton, *The Administration of the County Palatine of Chester, 1442–85* (Manchester: Manchester University Press, 1991), pp. 152–3.

3. *Harl. 433*, II, p. 197.

4. J. C. Wedgwood, *History of Parliament*, vol. 2: *Biographies of Members of the Commons House, 1439–1509* (London: HMSO, 1936), pp. 620–21 (Mytton).

5. *Harl. 433*, III, pp. 124–8.

6. Ibid., II, pp. 228–9; *Crowland*, pp. 176–9; *The Manuscripts of His Grace the Duke of Rutland*, vol. 1, Historical Manuscripts Commission (London: HMSO, 1888), pp. 7–8.

7. Norman Davis (ed.), *Paston Letters and Papers of the Fifteenth Century*, Part 2 (Oxford: Oxford University Press, 2004), no. 801; J. Alban, 'The Will of a Norfolk Soldier at Bosworth', *The Ricardian*, 22 (2012), p. 7.

8. Attreed, I, p. 367.

9. Ibid., pp. 7–8; *Testamenta Eboracensia*, vol. 3, ed. J. Raine, Surtees Society, 45 (Durham: George Andrews & Co., 1864), p. 305.

10. *Crowland*, p. 179; cited by M. Bennett, *The Battle of Bosworth* (Gloucester: Alan Sutton, 1985), appendix 3.

11. Wedgwood, *History of Parliament*, II, pp. 74–5.

12. Vergil, pp. 218–19.

13. The story first appears in Edward Hall, *Union of the Two Noble Families of Lancaster and York* (1550), cited in Bennett, *The Battle of Bosworth*, p. 169.

14. *Harl. 433*, III, p. 125.

15. M. Axton and J. C. Carley (eds), *'Triumphs of English': Henry Parker, Lord Morley* (London: British Library, 2000), appendix 7, p. 262.

16. Crowland, p. 183; Vergil, p. 221; Bennett, *Bosworth*, p. 120.

17. G. Foard and A. Curry, *Bosworth 1485: A Battlefield Rediscovered* (Oxford: Oxbow Books, 2013), pp. 58–9, 188; Ross, *Richard III*, makes a similar point: pp. 221–2.

18. *Crowland*, p. 183; for a summary of other contemporary reports, including Molinet's, see Bennett, *The Battle of Bosworth*, appendices 2–3.

19. M. Pitts, *Digging for Richard III: How Archaeology Found the King* (London: Thames & Hudson, 2014), pp. 174–82.

20. Rymer (ed.), *Foedera*, XII, pp. 204–5; *PROME*, XV, p. 15; *Harl. 433*, III, p. 139.

21. *PROME*, XV, pp. 361–8.

22. *Harl. 433*, I, pp. 134, 169.

23. J. Weever, *Ancient Funerall Monuments* (London: T. Harper, 1631), pp. 648–9.

24. Axton and Carley (eds), *'Triumphs of English'*, p. 262.

Further Reading

The fullest biography of Richard III is now that of Michael Hicks, *Richard III: The Self-Made King* (New Haven, CT, and London: Yale University Press, 2019), which largely supersedes the earlier volume about him in the same English Monarchs series by Charles Ross, *Richard III* (London: Eyre Methuen, 1981). Professor Hicks is also the author of two shorter works on the king: *Richard III: The Man Behind the Myth* (London: Collins & Brown, 1991) and *Richard III* (Stroud: Tempus, 2000). A. J. Pollard's *Richard III and the Princes in the Tower* (Stroud: Sutton Publishing, 1991) ranges more widely across Richard's career than the title implies and is very well illustrated, as is the following book by the same author: *The Worlds of Richard III* (Stroud: Tempus, 2001), which focuses on Richard as northerner. The multi-authored *Richard III: A Medieval Kingship* (London: Collins & Brown, 1993), edited by John Gillingham, offers an authoritative and readable introduction to various aspects of the king and his reign.

Richard III has always divided historians. While most recent writers have steered a careful middle path, his quincentenary in 1983 produced two books avowedly at the opposite ends of the spectrum: Jeremy Potter's *Good King Richard? An Account of Richard III and His Reputation, 1483–1983* (London: Constable, 1983) and Desmond Seward's *Richard III: England's Black Legend* (London: Country Life, 1983).

A number of books look at particular facets of the king and his career. The 1483 rebellion is the subject of Louise Gill's *Richard III and Buckingham's Rebellion* (Stroud: Sutton Publishing, 1999). Michael Bennett, *The Battle of Bosworth* (Gloucester: Alan Sutton, 1985), sets the battle in the context of the reign and includes a useful appendix of contemporary accounts. Glenn Foard and Anne Curry, *Bosworth 1485: A Battlefield Rediscovered* (Oxford: Oxbow Books, 2013), is largely about the archaeology of the battlefield but has two useful sections on the historical perspective. Richard's religion is discussed by Anne Sutton and Livia Visser-Fuchs in *The Hours of Richard III* (Stroud: Sutton Publishing, 1996), a generously illustrated discussion of the king's surviving book of hours. A more general account is that of Jonathan Hughes, *The Religious Life of Richard III: Piety and Prayer in the North of England* (Stroud: Sutton Publishing, 1997). The role of service to the crown in Richard's reign is explored by Rosemary Horrox in *Richard III: A Study of Service* (Cambridge: Cambridge University Press, 1989).

A number of the contemporary sources for the reign have been translated. Among them are the two key chronicles: Dominic Mancini's *The Usurpation of Richard III*, edited by C. A. J. Armstrong, 2nd edn (Oxford: Clarendon Press, 1969), and the anonymous *Crowland Chronicle Continuations 1459–1486*, edited by Nicholas Pronay and John Cox (London: Richard III and Yorkist History Trust, 1986). *Richard III: The Road to Bosworth Field*, edited by P. W. Hammond and Anne F. Sutton (London: Constable, 1985), tells the story through a range of contemporary material. The same editors are responsible for *The Coronation of Richard III: The Extant Documents* (Gloucester and New York: Alan Sutton and St Martin's Press, 1983), which gives useful biographical sketches for all the individuals mentioned. Sean Cunningham, *Richard III: A Royal Enigma* (Kew, Richmond: National Archives, 2003), provides a brief account of Richard's career illustrated by photographs and transcripts of documents relating to the reign.

Picture Credits

Index